LEGAL RESEARCH AND WRITING

PROBLEMS AND EXERCISES

MICHAEL D. MURRAY
UNIVERSITY OF ILLINOIS COLLEGE OF LAW

CHRISTY HALLAM DESANCTIS
GEORGE WASHINGTON UNIVERSITY LAW SCHOOL

FOUNDATION PRESS

395 Hudson Street
New York, NY 10014
Phone Toll Free 1–877–888–1330
Fax (212) 367–6799
fdpress.com

Printed in the United States of America

ISBN 1–58778–900–0

TEXT IS PRINTED ON 10% POST CONSUMER RECYCLED PAPER

Part I
Problems and Exercises

Appendix A
PREPARING A CASE BRIEF OR CASE ANALYSIS FOR CLASS

CASE BRIEFING EXERCISE

Write a case brief of the following judicial opinion:

Jo Ann NELSON, by her father and next friend, Eric D. Nelson, Plaintiff-Appellant,

v.

George N. LEWIS, Defendant-Appellee.

No. 75--432.
Appellate Court of Illinois, Fifth District.
March 3, 1976.

Plaintiff, by her father and next friend, brought action under dog bite statute for injuries inflicted upon her by defendant's dog. The Circuit Court, St. Clair County, Robert L. Gagen, J., rendered judgment in favor of defendant, and plaintiff appealed. The Appellate Court, Karns, P.J., held that "provocation" within meaning of dog bite statute means either intentional or unintentional provocation, that defendant's dog was provoked by plaintiff's unintentional acts and did not viciously react to those acts, and that thus plaintiff was precluded from recovering.

Affirmed.

Fleming & Fleming, O'Fallon, for plaintiff-appellant.

Brady, Donovan & Hatch, By Vincent J. Hatch, Belleville, for defendant-appellee.

KARNS, Presiding Justice.

Plaintiff, by her father and next friend, brought an action under the Illinois "dog-bite" statute (Ill.Rev.Stat.1973, ch. 8, par. 366) for injuries inflicted upon her by defendant's dog. From judgment entered on a jury verdict for the defendant, she appeals.

On the date of her injury, plaintiff Jo Ann Nelson, a two and a half year old, was playing "crack-the-whip" in defendant's backyard with his daughter and other children. Jo Ann was on the end of the "whip." The testimony shows that after she had been thrown off the whip, Jo Ann fell or stepped on the dog's tail while the dog was chewing a bone. The dog, a large Dalmatian, reacted by scratching the plaintiff in her left eye. There was no evidence that plaintiff or anyone else had teased or aggravated the dog before the incident, nor was there evidence that the dog had ever scratched, bitten, or attacked anyone else. According to its owner, the dog had not appeared agitated either before or after the incident. As a result of her injuries, Jo Ann incurred permanent damage to a tear duct in her left eye. It was established that Jo Ann's left eye will overflow with tears more frequently and as a result of less irritation than normal, but that her vision in the eye was not affected.

[1] Our statute pertaining to liability of an owner of a dog attacking or injurying {sic} persons provides:

> If a dog or other animal without provocation, attacks or injures any person who is peacefully conducting himself in any place where he may lawfully be, the owner of such dog or other animal is liable in damages to such person for the full amount of the injury sustained. Ill. Rev. Stat. 1973, ch. 8, par. 366.

Under this statute there are four elements that must be proved: injury caused by a dog owned or harbored by the defendant; lack of provocation; peaceable conduct of the person injured; and the presence of the person injured in a place where he has a legal right to be. Siewerth v. Charleston, 89 Ill.App.2d 64, 231 N.E.2d 644 (1967); Messa v. Sullivan, 61 Ill.App.2d 386, 209 N.E.2d 872 (1965); Beckert v. Risberg, 50 Ill.App.2d 100, 199 N.E.2d 811 (1964) Rev'd on other grounds 33 Ill.2d 44, 210 N.E.2d 207 (1965). There is no dispute but that the dog caused the plaintiff's injury; the defendant owned the dog; the plaintiff's conduct was peaceable; and she was injured in a place where she had a legal right to be. The issue presented is whether plaintiff's unintentional act constitutes "provocation" within the meaning of the statute.

[2] It appears that this issue has not been passed upon by an Illinois court. The statute does not distinguish between intentional and unintentional acts of provocation and thus, defendant argues, an unintentional act, so long as it provokes an animal or dog, may constitute provocation. Defendant's position, that the mental state of the actor who provokes a dog is irrelevant is consistent with the commonly understood meaning of provocation. Provocation is defined as an act or process of provoking, stimulation or incitement. Webster's Third New International Dictionary. Thus it would appear that an unintentional act can constitute provocation within the plain meaning of the statute.

Only three reported decisions have considered the question of provocation within the meaning of this statute. In Siewerth v. Charleston, supra, the court held there was provocation where the injured boy and his companion kicked a dog three times. The argument was there raised that provocation meant only an intentional act, but the court did not pass upon this contention as it found the injured boy's acts in kicking the dog clearly intentional and provoking. In Messa v. Sullivan, supra, the court found no provocation on the part of the plaintiff where she walked into a hallway patrolled by a watch dog that attacked her on sight. The court held the acts of the plaintiff did not constitute provocation within the intent of the statute and that plaintiff had a right to be on the defendant's premises.

While plaintiff argues that in Messa the plaintiff did not intend to provoke the dog and there was no provocation found, it appears that the court's holding was based on a determination that plaintiff's actions and conduct were not of a provoking nature, not on any determination of the intent with which plaintiff's acts were done. The court stated that it did not believe "provocation" within the meaning of the statute was intended to apply to a situation where a vicious dog interpreted a visitor's nonthreatening movements as hostile actions calling for attack. Similarly in Steichman v. Hurst, 2 Ill.App.3d 415, 275 N.E.2d 679 (1971), it was held that the acts of a postal carrier in spraying the defendant's dog with a repellant was not provocation. Although language in the decision might be read to mean that absence of intent by the plaintiff to provoke is material, we do not believe that this is an accurate reading of the opinion. In Steichman the letter carrier had previous difficulties with defendant's dog and had made several efforts to avoid the dog on the day she was attacked. The court characterized her conduct as "reasonable measures for self protection evoked by the dog's actions and deterring him only momentarily." Thus, the plaintiff's acts, although intentional, did not amount to an incitement or provocation of the dog, triggering the attack.

[3] In the present case, it was admitted that the plaintiff jumped or fell on the dog's tail; that the dog was of a peaceful and quiet temperament; and that the dog was gnawing on a bone when the incident occurred. Under these circumstances, we believe that the dalmatian was provoked, although the provocation was not intentional.

Plaintiff argues that since her act was unintentional, or that because she was of an age at which she could not be charged with scienter, she did not provoke the dog within the meaning of the act. Although her counsel presents a strong argument for interpreting the instant statute to impose essentially strict liability upon a dog owner for injuries caused to a child of tender years, we cannot agree that the public policy of this State compels the adoption of such a standard.

[4] At common law in Illinois, one injured by a dog could recover from the owner only if he could prove that the dog had manifested a disposition "to bite mankind" and that the dog's keeper or owner had notice of this disposition. Chicago and Alton Railroad Co. v. Kuckkuck, 197 Ill. 304, 64 N.E. 358 (1902); Domm v. Hollenbeck, 259 Ill. 382, 102 N.E. 782 (1913); Klatz v. Pfeffer, 333 Ill. 90, 164 N.E. 224 (1928). He could not recover for an injury resulting from his own contributory negligence either by knowingly exposing himself to the dangerous dog (Chicago and Alton Railroad Co. v. Kuckkuck, supra) or by provoking the dog. Keightlinger v. Egan, 65 Ill. 235 (1872). A dog owner's liability rested upon negligence, and he could be liable only if he harbored a "vicious" dog. Thus, one injured by a dog bore a substantial burden of proof.

[5][6][7][8] The instant statute, and its immediate predecessor, substantially eased this

burden imposed by the common law. It eliminates the requisite proof that the dog was vicious towards humans and that the owner knew of this disposition, and made irrelevant questions of the injured person's contributory negligence (other than provocation). Beckert v. Risberg, 33 Ill.2d 44, 210 N.E.2d 207 (1965). We do not believe, however, that it was meant to impose strict liability on dog owners for all injuries caused by dogs, except those intentionally provoked. Instead this act was apparently drawn to eliminate as much as possible any inquiry into subjective considerations. Whether the injured person was attacked or injured while conducting himself in a peaceful manner in a place where he could lawfully be are all matters which require no inquiry into a person's intent. We believe that the determination of "provocation" should also be made independently of such considerations. A determination of provocation does not require consideration of the degree of wilfullness which motivates the provoking cause. Had the legislature intended only intentional provocation to be a bar to recovery we think it would have so specified. Its conclusion apparently was that an owner or keeper of a dog who would attack or injure someone without provocation should be liable. This implies that the intent of the plaintiff is immaterial. Nor do we think that the plaintiff's status as a child of tender years should relieve her of all responsibility for a provoking act. Our Supreme Court in Beckert v. Risberg, 33 Ill.2d 44, 210 N.E.2d 207 (1965), sanctioned a jury instruction in the language of the statute where the plaintiff was a three year old boy. Although the court did not specifically address the issue, it appears by implication that a young child is not exempted from responsibility for his or her acts which provoke a dog under this statute.

We have been referred to decisions from other jurisdictions which permit an injured person to recover for unintentional acts which "provoke" a dog. Two of these cases, however, were decided on common law negligence theories, the courts concluding that these unintentional acts did not constitute contributory negligence. Smith v. Pelah, 2 Strange 1264, 93 Eng.Rep. 1171 (1795); Fake v. Addicks, 45 Minn. 37, 47 N.W. 450 (1890). Another case applied a statute which provided for strict liability for injuries inflicted by a dog unless the injury was voluntarily brought on by plaintiff with full knowledge of the probable consequences. Wojewoda v. Rybarczyk, 246 Mich. 641, 225 N.W. 555 (1929). These decisions are inapposite in that while they arise from similar factual situations they were decided upon legal theories which placed emphasis upon the injured person's scienter.

[9] Although we believe that the instant statute does not impose liability upon a dog owner whose animal merely reacts to an unintentionally provocative act, the present appeal does not involve a vicious attack which was out of all proportion to the unintentional acts involved. E.g. Messa v. Sullivan, supra. The dalmatian here apparently only struck and scratched plaintiff with a forepaw in response to the plaintiff's stepping or falling on its tail while it was gnawing on a bone, an act which scarcely can be described as vicious. Therefore we hold that "provocation" within the meaning of the instant statute means either intentional or unintentional provocation; that the defendant's dog was provoked by the plaintiff's unintentional acts and did not viciously react to these acts; and that no reversible error was committed in the trial court.

For the foregoing reasons, the judgment of the Circuit Court of St. Clair County is affirmed.

AFFIRMED.

JONES and GEORGE J. MORAN, JJ., concur.

Chapter 1
INTRODUCTION TO THE PROCESS OF LAW

QUESTIONS FOR DISCUSSION AND REVIEW

1. Identify your citizenship relationships. What municipality, village, or township do you live in? What county? What state? What are the legislative, executive and judicial entities called in these areas?

2. What are the three main primary sources of the law?

3. When can secondary authority define the law of a given area?

4. Do the following sources sound like primary or secondary sources of the law? Explain why:

   Aldermanic decree

   Corpus Juris Secundum legal encyclopedia

   Environmental Protection Agency regulation

   Congressional subcommittee report on pending legislation

   Farnsworth's treatise on Contracts

   McKinney's Consolidated Laws of New York Annotated

Chapter 2
RULES OF LAW AND LEGAL REASONING

QUESTIONS FOR DISCUSSION AND REVIEW

1. What is the difference between a rule of law with three required elements and one that has a balancing test?

2. Authorities always state rules of law in outline form—true or false?

3. Rule-based reasoning is the basic logical form used in legal writing, but how can the other forms of argument be used to buttress the legal conclusions you are communicating?

4. Where is narrative reasoning most often employed in legal writing?

5. When might a policy-based argument be the only argument you raise?

6. Why is analogical reasoning of special importance in England and the United States?

WRITING EXERCISES

1. Break down the following rules into an outline of the elements or factors. In brackets that follow each rule, we have suggested the number of elements that the rule should be broken down into:

    A. Every person who, under color of any statute, ordinance, regulation, custom, or usage, of any State or Territory or the District of Columbia, subjects, or causes to be subjected, any citizen of the United States or other person within the jurisdiction thereof to the deprivation of any rights, privileges, or immunities secured by the Constitution and laws, shall be liable to the party injured in an action at law. 42 U.S.C. § 1983 (1994). [2 elements]

B. Summary judgment shall be rendered forthwith if the pleadings, depositions, answers to interrogatories, and admissions on file, together with the affidavits, if any, show that there is no genuine issue as to any material fact and that the moving party is entitled to a judgment as a matter of law. Fed. R. Civ. P. 56(c). [2 elements]

C. To have standing, a party must show that he personally has suffered some actual or threatened injury as a result of the putatively illegal conduct of the defendant, and that the injury fairly can be traced to the challenged action and is likely to be redressed by a favorable decision. <u>See</u> <u>Valley Forge Christian College v. Americans United for Separation of Church and State, Inc.</u>, 454 U.S. 464, 472 (1982). [4 elements]

D. Any person, having the intent to commit a felony, assault or theft therein, who, having no right, license or privilege to do so, enters an occupied structure, such occupied structure not being open to the public, or who remains therein after it is closed to the public or after the person's right, license or privilege to be there has expired, or any person having such intent who breaks an occupied structure, commits burglary. Iowa Code § 713.1 (1999). [5 elements]

2. Assume the basic rule on dog-bite liability in Apex is: (1) defendant's ownership of the dog; (2) injury caused by the dog; and (3) lack of provocation of the dog by the plaintiff.

There are three cases in Apex dealing with dog bite liability:

<u>Case 1</u>: Seven year old boy was on a neighbor's porch grabbing and pulling the ears of the neighbor's dog and poking the dog in the stomach. The boy was told several times by the neighbor to stop what he was doing and leave, but the boy continued until the dog bit him once on the cheek. The court held that the dog's owner was not liable for the damage caused by the dog because: (a) the boy had no right to remain on the neighbor's property; (b) the dog had a right to defend itself; and (c) even though the boy was a minor, he still

provoked the attack.[1]

Case 2: Three year old girl was playing jump rope on a neighbor's front porch near the neighbor's dog. She accidentally jumped on dog's tail. The dog yelped and scratched the girl on her leg with its front paws. The court held that the dog owner is not liable for the dog's attack because: (a) even unintentional acts can constitute provocation of a dog; and (b) the attack was proportionate to the amount of provocation.[2]

Case 3: Door to door salesman, age 29, was going from house to house selling magazine subscriptions. He climbed up the front steps to dog owner's house. There was no dog in sight. As soon as he rang the bell, a dog jumped out and barked at him menacingly. He tried to move off the porch, but the dog followed his every move and was blocking him from leaving. The salesman sprayed the dog with pepper spray, which only partially hit the dog, and the dog jumped on the salesman and bit him several times before the man could run off. The court held that the dog owner was liable for the salesman's injuries because: (a) the salesman was using public sidewalks and going about his lawful business in a peaceful way prior to dog's attack; (b) the spraying of the dog with pepper spray was only undertaken after the salesman was trapped by the dog; and (c) use of pepper spray or other action taken purely in self-defense did not constitute provocation.[3]

A. Consider the following set of facts:

Client was returning to a party to retrieve his car keys. He had consumed a little alcohol at the party. It was past 1:00 a.m., and it was dark on the street where he had been at the party. The houses on the street were very similar in appearance. Client walked around to the back of a house where he thought the party was going

---

1 Based on Siewerth v. Charleston, 231 N.E.2d 644 (Ill. App. Ct. 1967). The Illinois line of dog-bite cases has proved fruitful for legal analysis. See Diana V. Pratt, Legal Writing: A Systematic Approach (1999); Robin S. Wellford, Legal Analysis and Writing (1997).

2 Based on Nelson v. Lewis, 344 N.E.2d 268 (Ill. App. Ct. 1976).

3 Based on Steichman v. Hurst, 275 N.E.2d 679 (Ill. App. Ct. 1971), and Dobrin v. Stebbins, 259 N.E.2d 405 (Ill. App. Ct. 1970).

on. It was the wrong house. In the darkness he tripped over a German shepherd sleeping behind the house. The dog got mad and bit client on the leg.

1. Draft a short statement of facts regarding client's situation employing narrative reasoning. Try not to add new facts, but you are welcome to elaborate on and color in or characterize the facts provided above.

2. Draft a short section employing rule-based reasoning which applies the Apex dog-bite rule to the facts of client's situation.

3. Draft one or two paragraphs employing analogical reasoning using one or more of the cases (Cases 1, 2, 3) provided above.

B. Consider the following set of facts:

Client accidentally threw a football into a neighbor's back yard. Client knew the neighbor had a large Doberman pinscher that normally was tethered in the front yard. He peeked over the fence and did not see the dog anywhere near his football. He jumped the fence, grabbed the football, and was running back to the fence when the dog came out from behind some bushes and ran over and caught client and bit him several times on the rear end before he could get over the fence.

1. Draft a short statement of facts regarding client's situation employing narrative reasoning. Try not to add new facts, but you are welcome to elaborate on and color in or characterize the facts provided above.

2. Draft a short section employing rule-based reasoning which applies the Apex dog-bite rule to the facts of client's situation.

3. Draft one or two paragraphs employing analogical reasoning using one or more of the cases (Cases 1, 2, 3) provided above.

Chapter 3
THE LIFE OF A CASE, STATE AND FEDERAL COURT SYSTEMS, AND JURISDICTION

Section I. THE LIFE OF A CASE IN CIVIL LITIGATION

QUESTIONS FOR DISCUSSION AND REVIEW

1. When a complaint is filed and served on defendant, what can the defendant do?

2. If a motion to dismiss is denied, what happens?

3. What is the response to a **reply** called? What is the response to this document called? Are you routinely able to file either one without special permission? What is that permission called?

4. Defendant filed a motion to dismiss and wants to notice up the motion for a hearing. Will defendant get a hearing? Why or why not?

5. What are the four major methods to discover information from your opponent in civil litigation? Explain how each works.

6. If someone is holding back documents and information from you in discovery, what do you do (after you tire of harassing them with incessant telephone calls)?

7. What are the two main elements asserted by the movant in support of every summary judgment motion?

8. When is an optimal time to file a summary judgment motion, and why?

9. What typically happens if a summary judgment motion is denied?

10. What is the primary reason for holding a trial? What is the difference between a bench trial and a jury trial?

11. If the jury enters a verdict against you, what options are open to you?

12. The loser in the trial court is called what on appeal?

13. In a typical civil case in this country, how many appeals are you entitled to as a matter of right?

14. What is a term that properly identifies the highest court in any jurisdiction? How would your case wind up in that court?

15. What happens if the appellate court reverses the lower court in a purely legal determination (i.e., concerning what the law provides or how the law is supposed to work in the situation at hand)? What happens if the appellate court reverses on the basis of one or more procedural errors?

Section II. STATE AND FEDERAL COURT SYSTEMS
and
Section III. HIERARCHY OF JUDICIAL AUTHORITY

QUESTIONS FOR DISCUSSION AND REVIEW

1. The Supreme Court of Texas can affirm or reverse the decisions of which courts and in what kinds of cases?

2. Can a judge ever overturn the decision of a justice?

3. What is the hierarchy of judicial authority above the Albany County Court in New York?

4. If you take an appeal from a decision of the Illinois Circuit Court, where might your appeal go?

5. If a state trial court of general jurisdiction in New Mexico is deciding an issue of New Mexico law, which courts' decisions potentially will be binding on this court:

   a. United States Supreme Court

   b. New York Supreme Court

   c. New Mexico Court of Appeals

   d. Alamogordo Municipal Court, New Mexico

   e. Chaves County Probate Court, New Mexico

   f. United States District Court for the District of New Mexico, Albuquerque Division?

6. If the Honorable Lester Ketterling is a District Judge of the District Court of North Dakota, Northeast Judicial District (a trial court of general jurisdiction), which courts' opinions is he likely to read most closely when he is researching how the courts have interpreted the statute Title 9, Chapter 9-06 of the North Dakota Century Code?

   a. Court of Criminal Appeals of Texas

   b. United States Court of Appeals for the Eighth Circuit

   c. Bismarck Municipal Court, North Dakota

   d. District Court of North Dakota, South Central Judicial District

e. District Court of North Dakota, Northeast Judicial District

f. Court of Appeals of North Dakota?

Section IV. JURISDICTION

QUESTIONS FOR DISCUSSION AND REVIEW

1. If a person is building a house outside the zoning board's jurisdiction, what does that mean? Which use of the term jurisdiction is this referencing?

2. A court might have jurisdiction over an action but not have venue. How can that be?

3. If a person constantly does business in Florida, but never steps foot there, what methods might a Florida court use to exercise jurisdiction over this person?

4. Sue is an artist who sues her landlord in the Maine District Court, District III, Bangor, for taking pictures of her artwork and selling the photographs in violation of her copyright. Before she knows it, her case winds up in the United States District Court for the District of Maine, Bangor Office. What happened? Can she add a claim to her complaint seeking the value of a painting that the landlord crushed when he slammed open the door to her apartment?

5. Ralph has a beef with his old buddy Norton for stealing food out of his icebox. Ralph would like to sue him in North Carolina, where Ralph now lives in retirement, but Norton still lives in New York City. One day, while having a beer at a bar across the street from the local airport, Ralph sees Norton walk out of the airport and cross the street and walk into the bar. The two former neighbors embrace and Norton tells the tale of his plane losing a section of the rudder forcing them to make an emergency landing at the airport. Ralph wastes no time in serving Norton with the North Carolina court's summons and complaint that he had with him, suing him for his past mooching. Norton says "Thanks a lot, Ralphie boy!" and storms out, and flies home on the next plane out. Based on these facts, can the North Carolina court exercise jurisdiction over Norton? If Norton wants to sue Ralph back for swindling him out of money in a futile scheme to renovate a hotel in New Jersey, what can he do, and where can he do it?

6. Jane moved from Manchester, England to Ohio, and opened a coke processing plant near the Ohio River in Cincinnati. She put it into operation on May 12, and almost immediately released a huge cloud of noxious fumes that drifted over the river and caused injuries to people strolling in Walker Park in Dayton, Kentucky. Jane is so distraught, she closed down the plant that same day, and never reopened it. She immediately retired to Arizona and from then on has never left her retirement condo. Based on these facts, can the injured parties in Kentucky sue her in a Kentucky court? Where else might they sue her?

7. Clara's homemade roach killer recipe was so effective that all of her neighbors wanted to use it. She slapped some handwritten labels on some mason jars and filled them with the roach killer and sold them to her friends and neighbors. One neighbor accidentally took a swig of the roach killer thinking it was the jar of corn whisky he had stashed under the sink, and suffered a serious injury. A friend tells Clara she better retain a lawyer that knows her way around federal law. Why did she give this advice?

8. Bobo is a citizen and resident of Cape Code, Massachusetts. He had his seaside newsstand destroyed by a crowd of tourists that swarmed the stand when it was rumored that Bobo had retrieved John F. Kennedy Jr.'s watch from the ocean and had it on display at the stand. Through diligent effort, Bobo determined that the tourists were citizens and residents of New York City, Boston, Philadelphia, Washington D.C., and Baltimore. Is it possible to sue all of them for negligence in one court? What about in a federal court?

Chapter 4
DETERMINING THE RULE FROM A SINGLE CASE OR OTHER AUTHORITY

WRITING EXERCISES

1. Read the following case and determine the borrowed rules, the applied rules and the holding of the case. Discuss any dicta that you think is noteworthy. Please note—this case is fictional. Any resemblance to people you know is regrettable:

---

768 W.2d 223

Daisy Mae DuBois, Plaintiff

v.

Abner Morton Heel, Defendant

No. 84CV1299-MDM

Circuit Court for Podunk County,
State of Apex

September 17, 1985

Counsel: Sylvester Chaser, Chaser & Ambulancer, P.C., Dogpatch, for Plaintiff.

Willkie Cave, Pompous, Boring & Whiteshoe LLP, Dogpatch, for Defendant.

Murphy, Judge:

Before this Court is plaintiff's motion pursuant to Local Rule 15 to separate and divide property in a common law marriage. The facts established at a one day trial on September 4, 1985, are as follows. Ms. DuBois ("plaintiff") and Mr. Heel ("defendant") have lived in the same house for seven years. They lease the house in which they cohabitate, and they stated on the lease that plaintiff and defendant were husband and wife. Both plaintiff and defendant signed the lease. The also signed loan documentation to purchase a 1978 Chevy pickup truck in August 1981 and a 1976 Harley Davidson motorcycle in March 1983. On each loan application they stated that plaintiff and defendant were husband and wife and both parties signed each loan. In 1980, defendant told a census taker that the plaintiff was his wife, that they were married for two years and that they lived together in the same household.

On November 22, 1984, defendant became enraged at plaintiff when she refused to let him pick and eat the skin off the Thanksgiving turkey. He threw his half-full beer can at her, which hit plaintiff and splashed beer on her clothing. A shouting match ensued, in which defendant proceeded to gather up all the empty beer cans out of the trash and pelt plaintiff with them until she fled the house. On the following Saturday, plaintiff attempted to return to the house to retrieve her clothing, but defendant "chased her out" by again throwing empty or partially empty beer cans at her. Plaintiff filed this suit on December 10, 1984.

Local Rule 15 states:

> If two persons living in a common law marriage separate following an act of aggression or violence by the common law husband against the common law wife, the common law wife may sue in the circuit court for a division of any property the two acquired during their common law marriage.

Rules of the Circuit Ct. for Podunk County (1982 ed.), Rule 15.

In Apex, it has long been recognized that a common law marriage exists between two persons if they:

1. Cohabitate;
2. For at least one year;
3. Hold out the other person as a spouse;
4. Have the intent or agreement to be married.

Pogo v. Dawg, 43 W. 234, 236 (Apex 1923).

In the instant case, there is no question that plaintiff and defendant cohabitated for over a year; both parties admitted that they lived under the same roof for seven years. Not surprisingly, the parties differ as to whether they held each other out as a spouse and had the intent or agreed to be married. In such a case, the courts refer to the circumstances of each individual case.

It is sufficient if the defendant has at least twice held out the plaintiff as his spouse. Here, the defendant concedes that he described the plaintiff as his wife on the lease for their house, and on certain loan documentation. These two instances satisfy the third element. The fourth element, intent or agreement to be married, may be shown by a continuous, monogamous relationship of the husband with the wife. It is not necessary to prove either party's state of mind so long as it is shown that the two lived in a monogamous relationship for an appreciable period of time. Seven years is certainly an "appreciable period of time." However, in this case we have additional proof of the husband's state of mind when he went out of the way to tell a census taker that he was married for two years to the plaintiff. Nothing in the facts of the case indicate that defendant had changed his mind about the plaintiff between 1980 and the date of their breakup.

Having determined that plaintiff and defendant lived in a common law marriage, we now turn to the portion of the rule requiring that their separation follow: "an act of aggression or violence by the common law husband against the common law wife." The threshold for this requirement is low; it is enough if any unwanted hostile act is attempted or undertaken by the husband against the wife. Certainly, defendant's two assaults and batteries against the person of the plaintiff are sufficient under this standard, however minor the damage inflicted may have been.

Plaintiff's motion for division of

property under Local Rule 15 is granted. The property at issue, two vehicles, are of roughly equal value. Plaintiff has requested an award of the Harley Davidson motorcycle, and this request is granted. Therefore,

IT IS HEREBY ORDERED, ADJUDGED AND DECREED that plaintiff shall take from defendant the possession and ownership of the 1976 Harley Davidson motorcycle identified in the complaint in this matter.

Chapter 5
DETERMINING THE APPLICABLE RULE THROUGH STATUTORY INTERPRETATION AND ANALYSIS OF MULTIPLE AUTHORITIES

QUESTIONS FOR DISCUSSION AND REVIEW

1. Your friend Bob is a student at Our Lady of the Lake University in Kit Carson County, Colorado. One night, he and three friends climbed the walls of the library and attempted to paint over the face of Jesus Christ depicted in the sixty foot high stained glass window on the front of the library. They wanted to replace the face of Christ with that of Tim Green, the star running back of the school who had just received the Heisman Trophy for that year. Just as they were getting started, one friend lost his balance and fell, but he was able to grasp the waistband of Bob's shorts. Unfortunately, as he slipped, he pulled Bob's shorts and underwear down to Bob's knees. As luck would have it, the Assistant Dean of Student Life, Msgr. O'Reilly, who periodically suffered from fits of insomnia, happened then to walk by the front of the library and saw Bob in all his glory swinging in front of the face of Christ. O'Reilly saw to it that Bob was charged with indecent exposure under Colo. Rev. Stat. § 18-7-302 (1999), in a criminal case filed in the District Court for Kit Carson County. (O'Reilly did not notice that the boys also were engaged in vandalism.) Bob's father has sent your firm a $15,000 retainer, and asked you to look into Bob's defense of the crime. Rank the following authorities in order of their value to your analysis of the law that governs Bob's situation:

    a. Smith case (1990), affirmed the conviction of a gas station attendant who refused to close his fly while working at a gas station. He was prosecuted and convicted for indecent exposure under Colo. Rev. Stat. § 18-7-302. The case was issued by the Colorado Court of Appeals, Division Three, the court that hears appeals from the District Court for Kit Carson County.

    b. Jones case (1957), affirmed the order of punitive dismissal of an officer who got into a "contest" involving outdoor urination with some of his junior officers at the United States Air Base at Aviano, Italy. The officer was punitively dismissed for conduct unbecoming an officer under Article 133, Uniform Code of Military Justice, 10 U.S.C. § 933. The case was issued by the United States Supreme Court.

c. Colorado Revised Statutes Annotated, section 18-7-302.

d. Rednape case (1998), affirmed the conviction of a window-washer who exposed himself to federal employees while hanging 15 stories up on the face of a federal building in Denver. He was prosecuted under 18 U.S.C. § 380043 (the language of which essentially is the same as Colo. Rev. Stat. § 18-7-302, but requires the exposure to take place on federal property). This case was issued by the United States Court of Appeals for the Tenth Circuit, hearing an appeal from the United States District Court for the District of Colorado.

e. Title 18 of the United States Code, section 380043.

f. Fletcher case (1977), affirmed the lower court's decision involving an indigent man who was robbed and beaten and left to wander naked in Vail, Colorado. He was prosecuted and found not guilty under Colo. Rev. Stat. § 18-7-302. The case was issued by the Colorado Supreme Court.

g. Fuller case (1994), affirmed the conviction of a woman who appeared topless in order to obtain necklaces of beads on the streets of Salina, Kansas, during a local Mardi Gras celebration. She was charged and convicted of the crime of common law indecent exposure. The case was issued by the Kansas Supreme Court.

h. Chapter 43, subsection D, of Prosser's treatise on Torts, discussing tort liability for indecent exposure.

i. Note, Criminal Liability for Indecent Exposure in Colorado, Utah, and Idaho, 97 Colum. L. Rev. 345 (1997).

j. E. Allen Farnsworth, Contractual Dysfunction and Indecent Exposure: Drafter's Liability for Debt Instruments under 15 U.S.C. § 3467, 25 Md. J. Contemp. Legal Issues 56 (1997).

2. Your client Mary does a mean Elvis impersonation. She was performing at B.B. King's Blues Club in Memphis, when she was served with process and enjoined under 17 U.S.C. §§ 501, 502, from selling reprints of movie posters of Elvis at intermission. Apparently, the works were copyrighted and she had simply purchased five posters and then made multiple color copies of them at the local Kinkos. Mary thought that because Elvis was dead, anyone could use pictures of him for commercial gain or profit. She has been sued by Graceland Properties, Inc. in the United States District Court for the Western District of Tennessee, Western Division. Rank the following authorities in order of their value to your analysis of the law that governs Mary's situation:

a. Sun Records case (1980), affirms a conviction for unfair competition under Tennessee law in a case involving the duplication and sale of copyrighted music recordings. The case was issued by the Court of Appeals of Tennessee, the court that hears appeals from the Circuit Court for Shelby County, Memphis, Tennessee.

b. Lewis case (1961), reverses judgment for plaintiff in copyright infringement case involving distribution of pirated recordings of Igor Stravinsky. The recordings were made by a college professor for use in lectures, and no commercial profit or gain was made by the professor from the recordings. The case was issued by the United States Supreme Court.

c. The U.S. Copyright Act of 1976, 17 U.S.C. § 101 *et seq.*

d. Cash case (1998), affirms judgment for plaintiff in copyright case in which defendant illegally taped country music star's concert and sold bootleg recordings over the Internet. The case was issued by the United States Court of Appeals for the Eighth Circuit.

e. Perkins case (1997), affirming a judgment against plaintiff for liability under the Visual Artists Rights Act of 1990, 17 U.S.C. § 106A, for mutilation of an artist's painting. The case was issued by the United States Court of Appeals for the Sixth Circuit.

f. Parker case (1994), where defendant was held liable for copyright infringement and unfair trade practices when he copied plaintiff's designs for western casual wear so as to produce clothing that was sold through catalog sales. The case was issued by the United States District Court for the Western District of Tennessee, Eastern Division.

g. Chapter 13, sections A-F, of the treatise Nimmer on Copyright (1998), discussing injunctive relief for infringement of protected works of visual media.

h. Melville B. Nimmer, Sources of the American Copyright Tradition in Elizabethan England, 57 Colum. L. Rev. 48 (1957).

i. Vol. 17, Corpus Juris Secundum, pp. 110-115, on copyright infringement. Corpus Juris Secundum is a legal encyclopedia.

WRITING EXERCISES

1. Read the following excerpts from cases and formulate the applicable rule for common law marriage in Apex, followed by any sub-rules on specific elements of the overall rule:

Pogo v. Dawg, 43 W. 234, 236 (Apex 1923) [Apex Supreme Court - the court of last resort in Apex] stated:

> In Apex, it has long been recognized that a common law marriage exists between two persons if they: (1) cohabitate; (2) for at least one year; (3) hold out the other person as a spouse; and (4) have the intent or agreement to be married.

DuBois v. Heel, 768 W.2d 223, 224 (Apex Cir. Ct. 1985) [trial level court] adopted the above rule, and went on to state:

> [T]he parties differ as to whether they held each other out as a spouse and had the intent or agreed to be married. In such a case, the courts refer to the circumstances of each individual case. It is sufficient if the defendant has at least twice held out the plaintiff as his spouse. Here, the defendant concedes that he described the plaintiff as his wife on the lease for their house and on certain loan documentation. These two instances satisfy the third element. The fourth element, intent or agreement to be married, may be shown by a continuous, monogamous relationship of the husband with the wife. It is not necessary to prove either party's state of mind so long as it is shown that the two lived in a monogamous relationship for an appreciable period of time. Seven years certainly is an 'appreciable period of

> time.' However, in this case we have additional proof of the husband's state of mind when he went out [of] the way to tell a census taker that he was married for two years to the plaintiff. Nothing in the facts of the case indicate that defendant had changed his mind about the plaintiff between 1980 and the date of their breakup.

Long v. Short, 745 W.2d 123, 125 (Apex Ct. App. 1st Dist. 1979) [Apex intermediate level appellate court] does not adopt the Pogo rule. It states:

> In order to demonstrate the existence of a common law marriage, plaintiff must show: (1) objective evidence of intent to be husband and wife, and (2) subjective evidence of intent to be husband and wife. Cohabitation, an appreciable length of cohabitation, and monogamy are regarded as objective evidence of intent to be married. A spouse's statements and representations concerning the status of the person he or she is living with are subjective evidence of intent to be married. It is a basic requirement of the claim that the couple must have commingled their finances — if the "wife" kept her paycheck and lived off of it by herself, and the husband did the same, there is no common law marriage.

Thin v. Stout, 812 W.2d 445, 448 (Apex Ct. App. 1st Dist. 1991) [Apex intermediate level appellate court]. Thin adopts the Pogo rule and cites DuBois, but the plaintiff-appellant ("wife") loses, even though the four criteria are met. In denying relief to the wife, the Thin court states:

> The husband and wife here were once legally and officially married, then divorced, and were subject to a divorce decree at the time that they started living together again. After the second time around went sour, the wife was thrown out, and then tried to go after half of the husband's property under the common law rule. This situation is not covered by the rules of common law marriage. A couple living under a divorce decree must abide by the terms of the decree, and neither spouse can avoid the decree by asserting a claim for division of property through common law marriage rules.

Chapter 6
ORGANIZATION OF LEGAL WRITING

WRITING EXERCISES

1. Identify the TREAT sections in the following writing sample. For example, Thesis on Main Issue; Application of Sub-Rule on Element (B); Sub-Sub-Thesis on Element (a).

   Where you have identified an Explanation section, indicate whether you think it is synthesized or unsynthesized.

   Hint: there are three elements at issue—peaceful conduct, lawful presence, and provocation. Each element has a sub-rule with multiple elements, all of which are at issue. One of the sub-rules has a sub-sub-rule with two elements, both of which are at issue.

   Please note: In the following dog bite example, the action takes place inside an apartment building. Thus, it differs from the general hypothetical we have been looking at in previous chapters.

   We have filled in the description of a few sections to help you get started:

ANSWER: We have filled in the rest of the labels:

[Thesis on Main Issue]	**I. DEFENDANT IS LIABLE FOR PLAINTIFF'S DOG BITE INJURIES**
[Rule on Main Issue]	In Texas, in order to prevail on a cause of action for injuries resulting from the attack of a dog, a plaintiff must prove: (A) defendant owned or harbored the dog; (B) plaintiff was peacefully conducting himself or herself at the time of the attack; (C) plaintiff was in a place where he or she had a lawful right to be; and (D) plaintiff did not provoke the dog into attacking. Timmy v. Lassie, 567 S.W.2d 123, 125 (Tex. 1995); Bobby v. Rin Tin Tin, 569 S.W.2d 789, 791-92 (Tex. App. 1997).
	A. Defendant owned the dog.
	Defendant admits that he owned and harbored the dog that caused plaintiff's injuries. Therefore, this element is not disputed in this case.
	B. Plaintiff was acting peacefully.

[Sub-Rule on Element (B)]

To be conducting oneself peacefully, one must be: (a) engaging in a normal day-to-day activity or business; and (b) not behaving in a loud and boisterous behavior in close proximity to a strange dog. Bobby, 569 S.W.2d at 792.

In Timmy, the plaintiff's claims were dismissed by the trial court for failure to state a claim, and this order was affirmed by the Court of Appeals, 562 S.W.2d 135 (Tex. App. 1993), and the Supreme Court. 567 S.W.2d at 125. Plaintiff Timmy had broken into the home of defendant by smashing a plate glass window, and had broken open several internal doors before encountering defendant's dog. The Supreme Court stated that "an illegal and violent destruction of property" violates the "peaceful conduct" rule. 567 S.W.2d at 124.

In Bobby, the Texas Court of Appeals affirmed the trial court's order of summary judgment against the plaintiff. 569 S.W.2d at 792. The plaintiff and several of his friends had broken into a house in order to throw an impromptu party at the absent homeowner's expense. The party was loud and raucous, and several neighbors called the police to complain about the noise. Plaintiff stumbled upon defendant's dog when he opened the door to the basement. The court denied recovery to plaintiff on the grounds that his conduct violated the peaceful conduct requirement because it was a criminal "breaking and entering" of the home and "a disturbance of the peace." Id.

In Mouse v. Pluto, 571 S.W.2d 13, 15 (Tex. App. 1998), the Court of Appeals again held that plaintiff's conduct must amount to a "civil breach of the peace" in order to fail the "peaceful conduct" requirement. Plaintiff Mouse and two of his friends had ridden their bicycles across the defendant's yard several times on a hot summer morning. Their action had disturbed defendant's dog a great deal, and eventually, the dog got loose and bit the plaintiff. Plaintiff prevailed at trial, and the Court of Appeals affirmed, stating that bike riding was a normal day-to-day activity for children, and was not sufficiently boisterous and noisy as to be a disturbance of the peace that would violate the rule. Id.

In the instant case, plaintiff Smith did nothing to breach the peace. She pushed open the door to defendant's apartment; she did not break it down or go in by smashing a window. Plaintiff's action cannot be characterized as a criminal breaking and entering. Compare People v. Butler, 543 S.W.2d 908 (Tex. 1988), with

[Sub-Thesis on Element (C)]

People v. Maid, 565 S.W.2d 234 (Tex. App. 1994). Her presence in the apartment was quiet and unobtrusive. Therefore, plaintiff Smith will not be found to have violated the peaceful conduct element of the Dog Bite rule.

C. Plaintiff had a Lawful Right to be in Defendant's Apartment.

In order to recover, plaintiff must show that she was not: (a) trespassing, or (b) exceeding the limits of an actual or implied license to be present at the site of the attack. Timmy, 567 S.W.2d at 125-26; Bobby, 569 S.W.2d at 792. Although traditionally listed as having two requirements, the "lawful presence" element is really a single requirement of "no trespassing," because "to be trespassing, a person must certainly have exceeded the limits of their license, if any," and "[i]f a person has exceeded the limits of their license, they are trespassing." Bobby, 569 S.W.2d at 792-93

Trespassing in Texas has never encompassed an accidental straying onto the property of another because of a mistake of fact. See Bears v. Goldilocks, 345 S.W.2d 988, 989 (Tex. App. 1943) (defendant's accidental entrance into plaintiffs' household because defendant believed it to be the home of her grandmother was held not to be a trespass); Sawyer v. Joe, 700 S.W.2d 348, 350 (Tex. Cir. Ct. Tamarac Cty. 1989) (accidental straying onto property in the dark is not trespassing). See Restatement (Second) of Torts § 7812 (1978) (same). It is the mistake of fact itself that grants to the person a limited license to be present, but only for so long as it is reasonable for the person to remain mistaken about their location. Bears, 345 S.W.2d at 989-90. This holding has never been altered or amended in Texas. See Hansel & Gretel v. Hag, 889 F.2d 345, 347 (5th Cir. 1994) (discussing the viability of the Bears rule).

Smith's situation is identical to that of defendant Goldilocks in the Bears case. Smith was mistaken about the floor she had gotten off on and about the identity of the owner of the apartment she was entering. There were no markings outside the elevator door to indicate the floor number, and defendant's door had no markings on it that might have clued Smith in to her mistake. This case is controlled by Bears, and Smith is entitled to recover in spite of her accidental entrance into defendant's home.

D. Plaintiff did not provoke Defendant's dog into attacking.

Under the Dog Bite rule in Texas, provocation means: (a) striking the dog, or (b) directly threatening the dog with physical harm; (c) so long as the dog's attack is not out of proportion to the provocation. Timmy, 567 S.W.2d at 125-26; Bobby, 569 S.W.2d at 792; Bears, 345 S.W.2d 988, 989-90.

[Sub-Sub-Thesis on Element (a)]

1. Plaintiff did not strike the dog.

Striking requires physical contact with the dog. Id. It is undisputed that Smith did not strike the dog.

2. Plaintiff did not threaten the dog.

Defendant has spent the most time attempting to refute plaintiff Smith's argument on the "threat" element of the rule on provocation. Defendant's effort is to no avail, because the definition of a "threat" to a dog under the law is: "a violent act or gesture directed against the dog that suggests that immediate physical harm to the dog is imminent." Timmy, 567 S.W.2d at 126; see also Bears, 345 S.W.2d at 990 ("plaintiff must threaten to cause severe and immediate harm to the dog itself").

[Explanation of Sub-Sub-Rule on Element (b) (*synthesized*)]

No Texas court has ever denied recovery to a plaintiff on the ground that a threat provoked the dog where the plaintiff was not armed with a weapon. Compare Rubble v. Flintstone, 580 S.W.2d 23, 27 (Tex. App. 1983) (recovery denied where plaintiff threatened dog with a club), and Thatcher v. Sawyer, 455 S.W.2d 45, 47 (Tex. App. 1978) (recovery denied where plaintiff threatened dog with a rifle), with Dilbert v. Dogbert, 798 S.W.2d 123, 126 (Tex. 1990) (recovery allowed where plaintiff yelled and gestured at the dog but was unarmed), and Van Pelt v. Brown, 566 S.W.2d 234, 237 (Tex. App. 1972) (recovery allowed where plaintiff waved blanket at dog, but was otherwise unarmed).

The Texas Supreme Court in Dilbert established that a plaintiff must have some means of inflicting immediate harm on the dog other that simply being armed with his or her own fists and feet. 798 S.W.2d at 126-27. A plaintiff's theat to pummel the dog with his or her fists is insufficient to exonerate the dog-owner from liability for the dog's attack. Id.

Smith did not threaten the dog with a weapon. Her gesturing with one index finger at the dog cannot be viewed as a threat of imminent, violent harm to the dog. Therefore, Smith did not threaten the dog within the meaning of the Dog Bite rule.

3. The Dog's Attack was Disproportionate to Smith's Actions.

"Proportionality" under the Dog Bite rule is defined as requiring that: (1) the nature of the attack and the (2) severity of the attack both must be in proportion to the injury inflicted or threatened by the plaintiff. Bobby, 569 S.W.2d at 792. Even if Smith were found to have threatened the dog, the dog's attack was disproportionate to any threat in terms of the attack's nature and severity.

1. The Nature of the Attack was Disproportionate.

[Sub-Sub-Sub-Rule and Explanation of Sub-Sub-Sub-Rule on Element (1) (*unsynthesized*)]

The Bobby court explained that the nature of the attack must be proportionate to the threat of harm against the dog. Id. In that case, a dog was slapped on its snoot by the plaintiff, and the dog responded by biting the plaintiff on the face and neck. This response of biting the vital areas of the plaintiff's body was held to be disproportionate to the striking of the dog's face with an open hand. Id.

Although no other Texas case discusses this element, the Texas Supreme Court in Smithy v. Jonesy, 123 S.W.2d 345, 347 (Tex. 1965), surveyed the law of Texas, Iowa, Illinois, and Arkansas, and determined that if a dog is struck by the hand or foot of a plaintiff, the dog may only respond by biting the hand, arm or leg of the plaintiff in an effort to subdue the plaintiff; otherwise the attack is disproportional.

In the instant case, the dog responded to a hand gesture, not a slap, and responded by biting the face, neck and arm of the plaintiff. The dog did not attempt to subdue the plaintiff. The nature of this response was disproportionate to the action taken by plaintiff prior to the attack.

2. The Severity of the Attack was Disproportionate.

Bobby establishes that the severity of the injury caused by dog's response to the plaintiff's action must be the same or less than

	the severity of the injury inflicted on the dog by the plaintiff. 569 S.W.2d at 792-93.
[Application of Sub-Sub-Sub-Rule and Thesis Restated as Conclusion on Element (2)]	Plaintiff Smith inflicted no injury on the dog. Therefore it is clear that the dog's attack on plaintiff was disproportionately severe. Plaintiff is fully entitled to recover damages for a disproportionately severe attack.
Thesis on Main Issue Restated as Conclusion	As discussed above, all of the elements of the Texas Dog Bite rule are established by plaintiff Smith. Smith is entitled to recovery from defendant for the injuries inflicted on Smith by defendant's dog.

2. Prepare an outline of the Theses, Sub-Theses, and Sub-Sub-Theses from the TREATs, Sub-TREATs and Sub-Sub-TREATs that would be required for the discussion of the legal issues described in the following fact pattern:

> You have a client who changed his name to "Warren Buffet" and moved to Nebraska. Shortly thereafter, your client received a large dividend check from Worldwide Widgets made out and addressed to "Warren Buffet." The address was not the same as your client's residence, and your client was well aware that he did not own any shares of Worldwide Widgets, but he cashed the check and kept the money all the same. The next month, another check arrived, and your client cashed it and kept the money. Now, your client has received a harshly drafted letter and several phone calls from Worldwide Widgets' lawyer demanding the money be returned. Your client wants to know if he can keep the money.
>
> The elements of the cause of action of Money Had and Received in Nebraska are:
>
> 1. Receipt of money;
>
> 2. by mistake;
>
> 3. under circumstances that render the retention of the money unjust.
>
> The rule has a separate sub-rule to determine each element:
>
> Sub-rule 1 - Money is "received" when:
>
> (a) currency, including (i) bank notes, (ii) bank drafts, (iii) wire

transfer, (iv) bearer paper, (iii) other legal tender;
(b) is transferred;
(c) by one person or entity;
(d) and accepted into the possession of a different person.

Sub-rule 2 - Mistake occurs when:

(a) the transferor knew or should reasonably have known of the correct recipient;
(b) the money is transferred to an incorrect recipient;
(c) the transfer was brought about by the transferor; and
(d) neither the intended recipient nor the incorrect recipient caused or contributed to cause the mistaken transfer.

Sub-rule 3 - The recipient's retention of the money is unjust if:

(a) the money has enriched the recipient;
(b) under all the facts and circumstances of the case and the principles of equity, the retention of the funds by the incorrect recipient is improper.

3. Your firm's client, Jones, age 23, was driving a rental car when it was pulled over by the police for speeding. The police officers noticed a clear plastic bag containing a large quantity of a white powder stuffed in the map pouch behind the passenger seat. When questioned about the bag, Jones claimed that he never saw it before and he knew nothing about it, but he had had two passengers on his trip and they might have left it there. The bag turned out to contain two kilos of cocaine. Jones is on trial with his two passengers as codefendants in a conspiracy case in which the defendants are alleged to have distributed drugs and used firearms in connection with drug offenses. Jones maintains that he has never had anything to do with drugs or guns and was not part of the conspiracy. The prosecutors wish to introduce photographs of Jones taken in his high school production of "Scarface: the Musical," in which Jones played the title role. The photos depict Jones handling huge bags of drugs, firing submachine guns, and at one point plunging his face into a huge mound of cocaine. The prosecution claims that the pictures are relevant, because they show Jones had great familiarity with drugs, weapons, and drug trafficking because of his "Scarface" performance. Your boss wants to exclude the photos on the grounds that the probative value of the photos is outweighed by the unfair prejudice to Jones that will occur if they are shown to the jury.

Federal Rule of Evidence 403 states in relevant part: "Although relevant, evidence may be excluded if its probative value is substantially outweighed by the danger of unfair prejudice." The Federal Rules of Evidence are the source of this rule, and they are applicable in this jurisdiction.

Your research has produced three cases from your jurisdiction that discuss and apply Fed. R. Evid. 403 that are potentially useful to this matter:

Case 1: Prosecution sought to use photographs of a defendant in a drug conspiracy case posing with his small children next to piles of methamphetamine, and sometimes brandishing weapons next to the drugs. The photographs were held admissible, because the probative value of the photos in showing defendant's active participation in the conspiracy (rather than defendant's assertion that he was a casual drug user, not an active participant) outweighed any unfair prejudicial effect caused by the photographs in persuading the jury to find the defendant guilty of the crime.[4]

Case 2: Prosecution was allowed to introduce multiple photographs of firearms, drugs, and drug paraphernalia seized from a site used by members of alleged drug conspiracy, including defendant, because the photos' probative value in showing the extent and nature of defendant's involvement in a far flung conspiracy to distribute drugs outweighed any unfair prejudicial effect of the use of the photos in persuading the jury to find the defendant guilty of the crime.[5]

Case 3: In drug conspiracy case, graphic photographs of defendant's wife's face after defendant allegedly beat her were held inadmissible, because there was no probative value in the photographs. No fact at issue in the drug conspiracy case was made more or less likely to be true by the introduction of the photographs, and the credibility of defendant's or his wife's testimony on any issue important to the case was not challenged or buttressed by evidence of the matters depicted in the photographs. The admission of the photographs presented a risk of unfair prejudice to defendant because they might stir the jury's emotions against him.[6]

Case 4: Photographs of apartments that were alleged to be "crack houses"

---

4 Based on United States v. Hester, 140 F.3d 753, 759 (8th Cir. 1998).

5 Based on United States v. Candelaria-Silva, 162 F.3d 698, 704-05 (1st Cir. 1998); United States v. Chambers, 918 F.2d 1455 (9th Cir. 1990).

6 Based on United States v. Hands, 184 F.3d 1322 (11th Cir. 1999).

located in the same building where defendant lived and which showed drugs and drug paraphernalia lying about were inadmissible in defendant's drug conspiracy trial. There was no evidence that defendant had ever stepped foot in any of the apartments depicted in the photographs, and there was a significant risk that the jury would mistakenly associate the things depicted in the photographs with defendant and prejudge him of the crime of which he was charged.[7]

A. Draft a statement of facts (1-2 paragraphs) for Jones's motion to exclude the evidence that employs narrative reasoning. Mention the background facts of the case and the facts concerning the photographs.

B. Draft a Thesis heading, Rule section, and Explanation section using the above cases.

C. Draft an Application section, again using the above cases.

4. Colorado law defines indecent exposure as the "intentional revealing of the genital area of one person to another person that is likely to be shocked or offended by such display."

A. Using the facts of Discussion Question 1 from Chapter 5 above, draft a statement of facts from Bob's perspective in defense of the crime.

B. Using the same facts, draft a statement of facts from the county prosecutor's perspective in support of conviction.

C. Draft an explanation section employing explanatory synthesis that is based on three or more of the cases provided in Discussion Question 1, a-j. Invent details for these authorities as necessary, but follow the format of a synthesized explanation section.

5. Federal law defines copyright infringement as the "unauthorized copying of a protected creative work." There is an exception to the rule for "fair use," and one such fair use is for "illustration and critique in an educational context."

A. Using the facts of Discussion Question 2 from Chapter 5 above, draft a statement

---

7 Loosely based on United States v. Akers, 702 F.2d 1145 (D.C. Cir. 1983).

of facts from Mary's perspective in defense of the lawsuit.

B. Using the same facts, draft a statement of facts from plaintiff Graceland Properties' perspective in support of liability.

C. Draft an explanation section employing explanatory synthesis that is based on three or more of the cases provided in Discussion Question 2, a-j. Invent details for these authorities as necessary, but follow the format of a synthesized explanation section.

Chapter 7
THE OFFICE MEMORANDUM AND THE CLIENT LETTER

WRITING EXERCISES

1. Change these issues (questions presented) to fit the pattern described in Chapter 7 to make them more helpful and meaningful to the reader:

   a. Whether photographs of "crack houses" in defendant Smith's apartment building are admissible?

   b. Whether the photographs of defendant Heel standing with his baby in font of bags of drugs is more probative than prejudicial?

   c. Whether Warner provoked his neighbor's dog to attack when he retrieved his football from his neighbor's yard?

   d. Whether Warner's neighbor's dog's attack on Warner was disproportionate to the provocation of the dog?

2. Change these conclusions (brief answers) to fit the pattern described in Chapter 7 (highlights of the relevant facts —highlights of the law—legal conclusions) to make them more helpful and meaningful to the reader:

   a. The photographs of "crack houses" in defendant Smith's apartment building are inadmissible under Rule 403. There is nothing to link Smith to the "crack houses."

   b. Yes, the photographs of defendant Heel standing with his baby in font of bags of drugs are more probative than prejudicial and are admissible under Rule 403. The photographs show that Heel knew there were drugs around.

   c. Warner provoked his neighbor's dog to attack when he retrieved his football from his neighbor's yard. He ran across the yard where the dog could see him, and any self-respecting guard dog would pursue and attempt to deter such conduct.

d. No, Warner's neighbor's dog's attack on Warner was not disproportionate to the provocation of the dog. The dog saw Warner as an intruder and had a right to protect the neighbor's property from a trespasser.

3. Change these thesis headings to fit the pattern described in Chapter 7 to make them more helpful and meaningful to the reader (and remember to include the "because" part):

a. The photographs of "crack houses" are inadmissible.

b. Photographs of Heel standing with his baby in font of bags of drugs are admissible because they are more probative than prejudicial.

c. Provocation of the dog by Warner.

d. Warner's neighbor's dog's attack on Warner was not disproportionate to the provocation of the dog.

Chapter 9
LEGAL CITATION

CITATION EXERCISES

Identify what is wrong (if anything) with the following citations. For your information, we have indicated the number of errors for each citation. Remember — spacing counts!

SERIES 1

1. Brownstein v. Morris, 203 N.Y.S.2d 465 (N.Y. App. Div. 4th Dep't 1990). [1 error]

2. The applicable standard is gross negligence. Smith v. Jones, 918 S.W. 2d 222, 224 (Mo. 1997). [1 error]

3. The evidentiary standard is one of gross negligence. Missouri Rev. Stat. §232.12 (1986); See Smith v. Jones, 218 S.W.3d 222, 224 (Mo. 2005); Huffy v. Carmichael, 846 S.W.2d 333, 345 (Mo. 1987). [4 errors]

4. The Illinois Dog Bite Statute, 510 Ill. Comp. Stats. section 5/16 (Smith Hurd 1996); defines a dog-owner's liability for a dog bite. [3 errors]

5. Dog bite liability requires a lack of provocation, See Ky. Rev. Stat. Ann. §§ 123 (1996); Norton v. Cramden, 354 Ky. 268, 270 (1946); Eckert v. Triesberger, 210 Ky. App. Rptr. 207 (Ky. App. 1965), but provocation can be offset if the dog is a hunting dog, Eckert, Id., or a dog trained to kill. Norton, Id. [8 errors]

6. The Erie doctrine confuses the issue of choice of law. Mast v. John, 75 Iowa 23, 24 (1988); see also Hill v. Willy, 866 P. 2d 433, 444 (OK. 1978) (discussing fact that Erie confuses most issues of conflict of laws, including forum selection.). [4 errors]

7. Car dealers must take reasonable care not to deceive buyers. cf. Cloff v. Decchor, 239 So. E. 2d 235, 237 (S.C. Ct. App. 1st Dist.) (jeweler required to take reasonable care not to deceive customer); Uy v. Hale Bopp Comet Company, 236 Ga. 457, 459 (1973) (similar). [5 errors]

8. If the shoe fits, a person will wear it. Compare Non v. Den, 432 Vt. 234, 236 (1990) (shoe fit, it was worn); and Ricky v. Mtz, 365 Vt. 245, 249 (1982) (shoe fit, it was worn); with Soby v. Sagy, 953 Vt. 988, 991 (1997) (shoe did not fit, it was not worn); and Hujey v. Quacker, 289 Vt. 656, 659 (1978) (per curiam) (shoe did not fit, it was not worn). [1 error]

9. The following paragraphs appear in the document:

> Red is used for anger. Rea v. Olena, 123 U.S. 234, 238 (1923). Blue is for peace. Id. Purple is for sorrow. Id. at 239.
>
> When writing, try to be colorful. Rea, supra, 123 U.S. at 239. It is the best practice in Missouri, because statutes require it. Mo. Rev. Stat. § 212.2, 212.6, 254.2. However, it cannot overcome a procedural defect. Id. § 212.2 *et seq.* [3 errors]

10. The Erie doctrine confuses the issue of choice of law. Masters, Inc. v. Johns, 55 N.W. 23, 24 (Minn. 1917); see also Hill v. Williams, 766 N.W. 433, 444 (Minn. 1918). It also confuses conflict of laws, id., including the law of forum selection. See Masters, Inc., id. at 25. [2 errors]

11. Mr. Roger Smith v. Mr. Jones' Washing Mach. Co., Incorporated, 12 S.W.2d 13 (Tenn. 1937). [2 errors]

12. State of Missouri in the relation of Jay Nixon, Attorney General v. American Tobacco Indus., Inc., 980 S.W.2d 233 (Mo. 1998). [2 errors]

13. Presy v. Weckston, 833 S.W.2d 222, 223, 224, 233-35 (TX. 1996). [1 error]

14. Which of the following is incorrect:

> N.Y. Gen. Constr. Law § 456 (McKinney 1989)
>
> N.Y. Mun. Home Rule Law 77(a) (Consol. 1990)
>
> N.Y. C.P.L.R. 8209 (Gould 1991)

15. *Roget v. Hammond*, 488 F.2d 745, 766 (2d Cir. 1958), *certiorari denied*, 354 N.Y. 347 (1958). [3 errors]

16. Certain *non-majority opinions* were criticized. *Tex v. Texas Horn Co.*, 357 Ark. 456, 468 (1948) (Simpson, J., dissenting) (emphasis supplied) (arguing for new rule in Arkansas). [Are there any errors?]

17. *Idaho Const.*, art. 2, cl. 1 [2 errors]

18. 3 Murray, *How to Write the Best Brief in the World and other Moot Points*, 23-24 (Random House 1999). [3 errors]

19. *Restatement (Second) of Conflicts of Law*, sec. 23 (ALI 1966) [3 errors]

20. C.H. DeSanctis, "The Real Life of Lawyers: No Fun, No Rest," 24 Harvard L. Rev. 245-46. [5 errors]

SERIES 2

1. Which citation is correct?

   Mr. Carne Asada v. Ms. Chili Relleno, 123 F.2d 34 (7th Cir. 1900)

   Asada v. Relleno, 123 F.2d 34 (7th Cir. 1900)

2. Which citation is correct?

   All you need is love, *Ono v. Lennon*, 34 N.E.2d 23, 24 (N.Y. 1979), love is all you need. *Starr v. McCartney*, 44 N.E.2d 55, 56 (N.Y. 1982).

   All you need is love; *Ono v. Lennon*, 34 N.E.2d 23, 24 (N.Y. 1979); love is all you need. *Starr v. McCartney*, 44 N.E.2d 55, 56 (N.Y. 1982).

3. Which citation is correct?

   You may say I'm a dreamer, *See* *Ono v. Lennon*, 34 N.E.2d 23, 24 (N.Y. 1979), but I'm not the only one. See Starr v. McCartney, 44 N.E.2d 55, 56 (N.Y. 1982).

You may say I'm a dreamer, see Ono v. Lennon, 34 N.E.2d 23, 24 (N.Y. 1979), but I'm not the only one. See Starr v. McCartney, 44 N.E.2d 55, 56 (N.Y. 1982).

4. Which citation is correct?

Monkeys and gorillas are primates. Stanley v. Newtron, 112 S.W.3d 123, 124 (Mo. Ct. App. E. Dist. 1990), quoting Clemens v. Scott, 11 S.W.3d 32, 33 (Mo. 1990).

Monkeys and gorillas are primates. Stanley v. Newtron, 112 S.W.3d 123, 124 (Mo. Ct. App. E. Dist. 1990), quoting Clemens v. Scott, 11 S.W.3d 32, 33 (Mo. 1990).

Monkeys and gorillas are primates. Stanley v. Newtron, 112 S.W.3d 123, 124 (Mo. Ct. App. E. Dist. 1990) (quoting Clemens v. Scott, 11 S.W.3d 32, 33 (Mo. 1990)).

5. Which of the following are proper introductory phrases?

See, e.g.,
Id.
Contra
See generally
See in addition
E.g.,
Egad
See also
[no signal]
But see
Accordingly
Compare . . . and . . . with . . . and
Cf.
Cg.
supra

6. Which of the following cites to constitutions, statutes, and secondary sources are correct?

Mo. Rev. Stat. § 367.123 (1999)

510 Ill. Comp. Stat. 5/16 (1996)

Ind. Code § 72.3 (2001)

U.S. Const. art. II, § 1, cl. 2

U.S. Const. amend. XIV

21 Charles Alan Wright & Arthur R. Miller, Federal Practice and Procedure § 1006 (2d ed. 1987)

Restatement (Second) of Torts § 14 (1979)

H.R. 3055, 94th Cong. § 2 (1976)

Fed. R. Evid. 401

Samuel D. Warren, The Right of Privacy, 4 Harv. L. Rev. 193, 195 (1890)

Vicki Hearne, Wise Men and Elephants, N.Y. Times, Feb. 21, 1993, § 7, at 28

Lynn Hirsch, The Misfit, Vanity Fair, Apr. 1991, at 158

7. Which of the following are proper abbreviations?

S.D.N.Y.

Mo. Ct. App.

F.Supp.2d

cert. denied

Ill. Ct. App.

Ala. (for Alabama)

Alaska (for Alaska)

appeal filed (for appeal filed)

certiorari dismissed

F. 3d

U.S. v. Jones

(U.S. Dist. Ct. E.D. Mo. 1990)

Cal.App.3d

Organ. of American States

W.D.N.C.

Colum. J. Transnat'l L.

Harv. Int'l L.J.

SERIES 3

1. What, if anything, is wrong with each of the following citations:

Dog v. Cat, 17 F.Supp.2d 14 (7th Cir. 2001)
Dog v. Cat, 17 F. Supp. 2d 14 (7th Cir. 2001)
Dog v. Cat, 17 F. Supp. 2d 14 (N.D. Illinois 2001)
Dog v. Cat, 17 F. Supp. 2d 14 (N.D. Ill. E.D. 2001)
Dog v. Cat, 17 F. Supp. 2d 14 (N.D. Ill. 2001)

2. What, if anything, is wrong with each of the following short form citations:

Long form: *Dog v. Cat*, 17 F. Supp. 2d 14 (W.D. Tenn. 2003)

Dog v. Cat, 17 F. Supp. 2d 14
Dog v. Cat, 17 F. Supp. 2d at 18
Dog, 17 F. Supp. 2d 14 at 18
Dog, 17 F. Supp. 2d 14, 18
Dog, 17 F. Supp. 2d at 18
Id.
Id. at 18

3. What, if anything, is wrong with each of the following citations:

Dog v. Cat, 917 F. 2d 14 (7th Cir. 2001) (Justice Cooper)
Dog v. Cat, 917 F. 2d 14 (7th Cir. 2001) (Judge Cooper)
Dog v. Cat, 917 F.2d 14 (7th Cir. 2001) (Judge Cooper)

Dog v. Cat, 917 F.2d 14 (7th Cir. 2001) (Hon. Cooper)
Dog v. Cat, 917 F.2d 14 (7th Cir. 2001) (Cooper, J.)

4. What, if anything, is wrong with each of the following citations:

Cop v. Robber 17 Cal.2d 14 (Cal. 2001)
Cop v. Robber 17 Cal. 2d 14 (Cal. 2001)
Cop v. Robber,17 Cal. 2d 14 (Cal. 2001)
Cop v. Robber,17 Cal.2d 14 (Cal. 2001)
Cop v. Robber,17 Cal. 2d 14 (2001)

5. What, if anything, is wrong with each of the following citations:

Cop v. Robber 88 S. Ct. 414 (U.S. 1988)
Cop v. Robber 88 S. Ct. 414 (1988)
Cop v. Robber, 88 S. Ct. 414 (1988)
Cop v. Robber, 88 S.Ct. 414 (1988)
Cop v. Robber, 525 U.S. 875 (1988)

6. What, if anything, is wrong with each of the following citations:

17 U.S.C.S. 107 (1976)
17 U.S.C.S. §107
17 U.S.C.S. § 107 (1976)
17 U.S.C.A. § 107 (1976)
17 U.S.C. § 107 (1976)

7. What, if anything, is wrong with each of the following citations:

765 Ill.Stat. § 1075/5 (1998)
765 Ill. Stat. § 1075/5 (1998)
765 Ill.Comp.Stat. § 1075/5 (1998)
765 Ill. Comp. Stat. § 1075/5 (1998)
765 Ill. Comp. Stat. 1075/5 (1998)

8. What, if anything, is wrong with each of the following statutory short forms:

Long form: Mo. Rev. Stat. § 1075.23 (1998)

Mo. Rev. Stat. § 1075.23
Mo. Rev. Stat. §§ 1075.23, 1075.24
Id.
Id. § 1075.24

9. What, if anything, is wrong with each of the following citations:

United States Const., Fourteenth Am.
U.S. Const., 14th Am.
U.S. Const., Amend. 14
U.S. Const., amend. XIV
U.S. Const. amend. XIV

10. What, if anything, is wrong with each of the following citations:

Murray, Explanatory Synthesis, 14 Colum.L.Rev. 24, 25 (1914)
Michael D. Murray, Explanatory Synthesis, 14 Colum.L.Rev. 24, 25 (1914)
Michael D. Murray, *Explanatory Synthesis*, 14 Colum.L.Rev. 24, 25 (1914)
Michael D. Murray, *Explanatory Synthesis* 14 Colum. L. Rev. 24, 25 (1914)
Michael D. Murray, *Explanatory Synthesis*, 14 Colum. L. Rev. 24, 25 (1914)

11. What, if anything, is wrong with each of the following citations:

Amer. Law Inst., *The Restatement (Second) of Torts*, § 14
The Restatement (Second) of Torts, § 14
Restatement (Second) of Torts, § 14 (1967)
Restatement (Second) of Torts, § 14 (1967)
Restatement (Second) of Torts § 14 (1967)

12. What, if anything, is wrong with each of the following citations:

House Resolution 3055, 94th Congress, section 2 (1976)
House Res. 3055, 94th Congress, § 2 (1976)
H. Res. 3055, 94th Congress § 2 (1976)
H. Res. 3055, 94th Cong. § 2 (1976)
H.R. 3055, 94th Cong. § 2 (1976)

13. What, if anything, is wrong with each of the following citations:

Senate Report No. 89-910, at page 4 (1965)
Senate Report No. 89-910, at p. 4 (1965)
Senate Report No. 89-910, at 4 (1965)
Sen. Report No. 89-910, at 4 (1965)
S. Rep. No. 89-910, at 4 (1965)

14. What does it report?

S.W. S.W.2d S.W.3d

F.R.D.

Ill. Dec.

Idaho

U.S.

Misc.   Misc. 2d

F.   F.2d   F.3d

Ill.   Ill. 2d   Ill. 3d

Cal. App.   Cal. App. 2d

Chapter 11
FEDERAL AND STATE REPORTERS OF CASES

RESEARCH EXERCISES:

SERIES 1

1. Who is the defendant(s) in the case cited at 221 F. 229? In what court does this case take place?

2. Properly cite the case cited in volume 771 of the Federal Reporter 2d Series p. 920?

3. In which case of the 181st volume of the Federal Reporter 3d Series has the Richland Parish Hospital as a party? Is the opinion of this case published?

4. Who was the district court judge in the case found on p. 337 of the 955th volume of the Federal Supplement? What is the style of this case?

5. What case is found on p. 1026 of the 867th volume of the Federal Supplement? Who are the intervening defendants?

6. Who was the appellant in the case located on p. 497 of volume 528 of the So. 2d?

7. On what page starts the case Autry v. Bryan in the 297th volume of S.E.2d? What day was the case decided? In what court was the case?

8. What judge wrote the opinion on p. 291 of the 505th volume of the P.2d? Who represented the Bauwens?

9. Of what was the appellant in the case cited 706 S.W.2d 664 found guilty?

10. What case is cited in the 665th volume of N.E.2d on p. 685? What parallel cite is given?

SERIES 2

1. Who represented Bessie McAfee in the case reported at 249 S.W.2d 822?

2. What is the style of the case reported at 389 U.S. 128? What are the parallel cites in the Supreme Court Reporter and in the Lawyers Edition reporter?

3. What New Jersey plumbing company is mentioned by name at page 696 in the 681st volume of the regional reporter that reports New Jersey cases?

4. On what page of the 115th volume of the N.W. reporter is the case involving Webster City Steel Radiator Company?

5. Find and properly cite the case styled South County Sand & Gravel Co., Inc. v. Town of South Kingstown, in the reporter which reports the decisions of the Federal Courts of Appeals.

6. What court rendered the decision in the case reported at 598 A.2d 580?

7. Which judge wrote the opinion at 598 A.2d 580?

8. Who represented Mary A. Ziehm in the Maine case reported at Volume 433, Page 725 in the regional reporter that includes Maine decisions?

9. Read the case at 201 P. 522. How old was Carney Varner when he testified in that case?

10. In Walker v. State, 153 P. 209 (Okla. Crim. App. 1915), where did Bessie Burgess believe she would go if she told a story and was a bad girl?

11. In Walker v. State, 153 P. 209 (Okla. Crim. App. 1915), on what grounds did the Court

find that the court below erred in refusing the defendant's request for a physical examination?

12. How does the Maryland Court of Appeals characterize the Maryland Rules of Procedure in Stewart v. State, 638 A.2d 754 (Md. 1994)?

13. What piece of machinery injured young Mr. Goza in 172 S.W. 825?

14. How did Texas Lawyer McKinney claim he came upon the stolen property found in his possession in McKinney v. State reported in volume 627 of the Texas regional reporter?

15. What did Samuel Robinson's attorney tell him would happen if he exercised his Constitutional right to a jury trial in People v. Robinson, 5 Ill. App. 3d 1065?

SERIES 3

1. Who is the first named defendant in the case cited at 221 F. 229? What court issued this opinion?

2. In which case of the 181st volume of the Federal Reporter, Third Series is the Richland Parish Hospital listed as a party? Is the opinion of this case published? Was this case affirmed or reversed?

3. Which district court judge wrote the opinion in the case found on p. 337 of the 955th volume of the Federal Supplement? Who represented the plaintiff, John Barone? What date was ordered by the court for a pretrial conference in the case?

4. On what page of the 297th volume of the South Eastern Reporter, Second Series does the case Autry v. Bryan begin? On what date was the case decided? In what court was the case decided? How many justices signed off on the opinion?

5. Using the key number digest in the back of the 665th volume of N.E.2d, what case on consumer protection is reported in the volume? What parallel cites for this case are given? On what date was rehearing denied in the case?

Chapter 12
CASE FINDERS AND VERIFICATION SOURCES: DIGESTS, ANNOTATED LAW REPORTS, AND SHEPARD'S CITATIONS

RESEARCH EXERCISES

In addition to writing down the answers, you should also write down the steps you undertook to answer the question. This should help you (and your professor) figure out where you went wrong if you get the wrong answer.

West Digest System Exercises

Series 1

1. What digest topic is categorized under key number 281? (Shame on you if you didn't check a pocket part for a digest to answer this one!)

2. If your case involves Indiana law, in what digest should you begin to search for Indiana cases? Does this digest report federal cases associated with Indiana from the United States Supreme Court, the U.S. Court of Appeals for the 6th Circuit, and the U.S. District Courts located in Indiana? If this digest was unavailable, in what other digest series could you find Indiana cases? If you wanted to find additional federal cases outside of the 6th Circuit as persuasive authority, in what other digest series should you search?

3. On the 4th of July, a child in Georgia was given some sparklers and firecrackers to play with by his father. He went off, unattended, to play with them near a neighbor's corn field and accidentally set the field on fire. According to the South Eastern Digest 2d, may the owner of the field in Georgia state a cause of action against the child's father for his child's use of common fireworks? Which 1965 Georgia case had facts that sound a lot like this client's facts? What Georgia Code sections are cited in the digest with this case? Under what digest topic and key number did you find this case?

4. An Iowa youth, Frank Benjamin, was fascinated by an exhibit he saw at a local science

center involving kite string and lightning. He decided to experiment with a kite of his own. Soon after takeoff, however, his kite became entangled in a much more terrestrial power source, the high tension power lines hanging over a field where children often fly kites. Frank is harmed and his parents want to sue. According to the North Western Digest 2d, which 1992 Iowa case discussed the duty of care required of a power company for lines installed in places where people are likely to come in close proximity to them? Under what digest topic and key number did you find this case?

5. According to the Pacific Digest (volumes beginning 101 P.2d), is it grounds for divorce in Kansas to fail to talk to your wife when you are tired, even if she considers it to be extremely cruel? Which 1947 Kansas case addressed this issue? Under what digest topic and key number did you find this case?

6. A client in Mississippi opened an ice cold refreshing Banjo Beer® and gulped down two swallows before he noticed a foreign object in his mouth. He discovered it to be a dead cockroach. Your boss thinks she read a Mississippi case from the mid-1950's to mid-1960's that involved a roach in a beverage and discussed the injuries associated with such an incident. In which edition of the Decennial Digest (9th, 10th, etc.) might you find this case? Which case is she remembering? (make sure it is a roach case) Under what digest topic and key number did you find this case

Series 2

1. Your little brother, Jim, fell off a park bench while playing tag with one of his friends. Your parents are planning on suing the city. Is there anyway the city will not be held liable for Jim's injuries? In what California case, cited in the 10th Decennial Digest, was the city immune from suit for injuries sustained in a city park caused from tree rope swinging?

2. Your son, Bill, decides to have a 4th of July party—same as every other year. During the firework display that he and his friends decide to put on for the neighborhood, the next-door neighbor's young daughter gets burned by one of the bottle rockets. What NY case in the 10th Decennial Digest has facts apposite to this situation and therefore you should read to help your son?

3. You are reading a Patricia Cornwell novel and become curious about fingerprinting and its uses to identify criminals. What case—in the 10th Decennial Digest—involved a crook who was identified by his palm print on a money order?

4. Use the 10th Decennial Digest. You and your fiancé have a huge fight. You think this might be the big one—you guys probably are not going to last. However, you like the ring he gave you. What cases established engagement rings as conditional gifts? What is the condition?

5. Tim is out golfing and accidentally slices a shot into the woods. Unknown to him, there is a homeless man sleeping in a tree and is struck, causing serious injuries, in the head. He thinks he could get some money by suing Tim. According to what 1993 Federal Kansas case, cited in the 10th Decennial Digest, is Tim not strictly liable for the man's injuries?

6. Your cousin, Larry, and his wife sought a divorce. Full custody of their six children was given to Larry's wife. Where does the Massachusetts Digest discuss child support? What Massachusetts case involves a duty to pay child support?

7. Is the death penalty legal in your state? What headnote numbers discuss the legality of the death penalty?

8. What 1992 Texas case is cited under headnote Criminal Law 1206.1(2) in the Texas Digest 2d?

9. Your friend, Sally, just turned 16 and thinks she is in love. Her and her new crush have decided to get married. According to the West Virginia Digest, can Sally get married in West Virginia at 16? What West Virginia authority established the age limitations on marriage in West Virginia?

10. Robby is in Daytona on vacation staying at the Sun and Beach Hotel. Early one morning he is running through the lobby to get to the beach and catch some rays when he slipped on the wet floor and hit his head. His parents are furious with the hotel and now they have come to you seeking a legal remedy. What case in the West's Illinois Digest discusses a hotel manager's liability when a guest fell due to "defective flooring"?

American Law Reports (ALR) Exercises

Series 1

1. You represent Kelly Berra. Better known to her adoring fans as Yeh-Yeh Apple. She is a New Orleans native, but internationally famous for her Latin dance performances. Ms. Apple headed down to Colombia South America this spring for a six-week national tour. She performed in hotel lounges and bars. The tour seemed to be a great success until one fateful April evening outside Cartagena. While Ms. Apple was performing at the Hotel Allende's pool side cantina, a small contingent of leftist guerillas laid siege to the entire hotel district. The rebels cut power and water supplies to the entire area and set up a perimeter with machine gun posts. The government responded quickly to this embarrassing incident. After two days of fierce battle with government forces, the rebels were turned back and the guests were able to leave their hotels. Ms. Apple headed straight for the hotel where she was staying to find that it had been used as the rebel's base camp. All of her belongings had been destroyed during the siege. Deeply troubled by her sudden bad luck, Ms. Apple hired transportation to the airport and caught the first flight back to New Orleans. She arrived disheveled, carrying only her gig bag. She was in a state of nervous shock after her traumatic experience. Upon arrival, a group of uniformed U.S. Customs agents approached her and detained her for three hours for questioning and search by drug sniffing dogs. Ms. Apple, who considers herself an honest, law-abiding citizen, wonders why she was suspected of being a drug courier. She wants you to explain the Customs Service's profiling system. Use only the ALR in answering the following questions: What article provides information on this subject? Who wrote this article? What Louisiana case is cited in this article?

2. Lori Vamos is a school bus driver in Santa Fe, New Mexico. The town has a large number of railroad tracks running through it. School bus drivers are required to stop at each crossing and look both ways before crossing the tracks. Lori always stopped at these crossings in the past, especially after a near-miss in 1984 caught the entire town's attention. Unfortunately, Lori is about to suffer her first attack of "Sudden Adult Onset Narcolepsy" ("SAON"). There is a test for SAON, but the Laredo Public School Authority ("Authority") feels that the test is too expensive since fewer than 1 in 70,000 people suffer from the disease. The Authority also believes that it would not be liable if there was a crash caused by their failure to test for SAON. What ALR article would provide information on the issue of the Authority's liability in this situation?

3. Fireworks fascinate young and old alike. Your client is no exception. Gary Sparks wants to open a new business called Mega-Fireworks Blowout. Gary has retained your firm to organize his business and to give him advice on the applicable state laws dealing with fireworks. What ALR 5th articles are there on local laws regulating fireworks? How many North Carolina statutes are listed in the ALR 5th article dealing with state fireworks

laws?

4. The Cardiac Jogging Society ("CJS") is a group of 20 heart attack victims who spend each Saturday jogging through the city park as part of their rehabilitation regime. Although all of them are in fairly good shape, they are under standing orders to avoid being startled by sudden loud noises or dangerous situations. Most of the members are in their early 60's. Byron Grave has just opened his dog walking service called Pexercise. As part of the Pexercise program, dogs are classed as to size and temperament and assigned to a trained Pexercise Guide™ who takes the dogs on their assigned route. Byron himself handles the dogs requiring the most expertise. He affectionately calls this group the A-Team. The 15 members of the A-Team are all 100 pounds or larger and include such breeds as German Shepherds, Great Danes, Giant Schnauzers, and Black Labs. On Friday, the A-Team was moving up the park bike trail in an orderly fashion when the CJS came suddenly around a steep bend in the trail, startling the members of both groups. Pandemonium broke out as the dogs began tangling their leashes around Byron and each other. One dog lightly nipped a CJS member on the calf. Two CJS members were taken to the emergency room with chest pains. Byron would like to know which ALR 4th articles are apposite to these facts. Is there a Wisconsin case discussing the owner's knowledge of their dog's viciousness before they can be held liable? What is its citation?

Series 2

1. Billy and some of his friends are having a BBQ to celebrate the 4th of July. Of course, they will shoot off fireworks. Billy wants to know the laws on buying and shooting off fireworks. What ALR 5th discusses laws regulating the sale, possession, use or transport of fireworks?

2. Who wrote the section found in question 1? What case is cited in this section?

3. You are sitting at your favorite restaurant when your sister begins choking on her chicken marsala. You are waiting for someone to help her when you remember you are certified in first aid and CPR. You save your sister. Two weeks later you are telling your heroic story to a friend and she asks about the duty of the restaurant or its employees in helping a choking customer. What section of the ALR 5th covers this topic? How many people choke on food each year in the United States? What is the duty of the restaurant, or its employees, to give to a choking patron and what case established this level of duty?

4. Your aunt, Isabella, is a famous Italian chef. She uses olive oil in everything—it's her secret ingredient. You are in the law library one day and decide to look up more about olive oil and any legal history it might have. What ALR Fed discusses olive oil? What case is featured in the ALR Fed on olive oil?

5. Your favorite home improver, Bob Villa, is doing a show on removing lead-based paint in residential settings. Before the show, you want to get a good background on this topic. What ALR Fed discusses the removal of lead-based paint and its cause of lead poisoning? What 1995 NY case is featured in the ALR Fed on this topic?

Shepard's Citation Exercises

Use Shepard's volumes to find the answers to the following questions. If the answers call for a case, give a full citation (style, citation, court, and date) for each case.

Series 1

1. What year 2000 cases have cited 45 S.E. 747? Cite each case.

2. What dissenting opinion cited 45 S.E. 466 Case 2? Cite the opinion.

3. What did 515 S.E.2d 565 do to the case at 470 S.E.2d 114?

4. What effect did 139 S.E.2d 898 have on 144 S.E. 547?

5. Your facts are similar to 494 S.E.2d 870. The holding is favorable to your client. Should you rely on this case?

6. You are downcast and forlorn. Your client is doomed! Her facts are on all fours with 379 S.E.2d 271. Is all lost?

7. Is 358 S.E.2d 160 still good law?

8. Have any federal cases cited Mo. Rev. Stat. § 351.633? If so, cite the first two cases.

Series 2

1. Did 720 A.2d 164 do anything to 602 A.2d 387?

2. What was the disposition of the case reported at 735 A.2d 9?

3. Did any Utah or Wisconsin cases cite 94 A.2d 34? If so, cite one case from each state.

4. What was the disposition of the case reported at 704 A.2d 81?

Chapter 13
SECONDARY SOURCES OF THE LAW: ENCYCLOPEDIAS, TREATISES, LAW REVIEWS, AND PERIODICAL INDICES

RESEARCH EXERCISES

In addition to writing down the answers, you should also write down the steps you undertook to answer the question.

Secondary sources - Overview

1. **Corpus Juris Secundum Legal Encyclopedia**

   Your client is an artist who submitted several paintings of nudes to a juried art exhibit sponsored by the City of Peoria, Illinois. Her paintings were rejected as "inappropriate" even though your client thinks they are far from obscene. Using Corpus Juris Secundum, what topic should you look under for guidance on the standards used to evaluate the city's decision?

   Under this topic, to what interest must the art appeal in order to be considered obscene? What U.S. Supreme Court case involving a west coast state lends its name to the test used to make the evaluation? What pre-1978 case discusses a Mississippi statute that was held to be invalid for overbreadth? What post-1978 U.S. Supreme Court case involving and arising in a midwest corn belt state discusses the concept that "most prudish or most tolerant" viewpoints are irrelevant in the determination?

2. **American Law Reports (ALR)**

   Using the ALR Quick Index, what is the citation of the ALR 3d annotation that discusses Baptist churches' property rights in disputes between local churches and parent church bodies? Who wrote this annotation? What court opinion is reported in this volume immediately preceding this annotation?

3. **Wright & Miller, Federal Practice and Procedure (West)**

Using the General Index and Tables covering volumes 1-31 (2004 ed.), what section of Wright & Miller's Federal Practice and Procedure covers Internet jurisdiction over nonresident defendants? In this section of Wright & Miller, what is the name of the 1997 Western District of Pennsylvania case involving a cigarette lighter manufacturer that the authors think is "the most influential judicial opinion thus far" on the topic of Internet jurisdiction? What kind of scale is used to evaluate categories of websites? According to the notes here, in what section of Wright & Miller, Federal Practice and Procedure would be learn more about this scale?

4. **Nimmer on Copyright**

Your great uncle was a fine musician and composer. After his death, a nearly complete score for a symphony was discovered in his piano bench. You wonder if he or his estate could claim any rights in the work. What section of Nimmer on Copyright discusses posthumous rights? What famous composer's case is discussed at great length in this section? What is the style of this composer's case? Was the trial court's opinion in this case reversed?

5. **Index to Legal Periodicals & Books and Law Review Articles**

Using the Index to Legal Periodicals & Books volume dated September 2001-August 2002, what is the title of the article written by Lori F. Damrosch in 2002 listed in the index? What is the citation given for this article?

Using the same index volume (Sept. 2001-Aug. 2002), what is the title of the article on Appellate Advocacy that involves a fish? Who is the author of this article? What is the citation given for this article? Looking at this "fishy" article in the actual bound volume for this law review, to whom is the author indebted for the vignette he quotes on the first page of the article?

Encyclopedia Exercises

Use the legal encyclopedias indicated in each exercise to answer the questions found therein:

Series 1

1. Where does the American Jurisprudence discuss fireworks and the sale to minors? What state prohibits the sale of fireworks to children under 12?

2. Your brother, Russ, wants to get married, but he does not want to hassle with a wedding ceremony or the justice of the peace. He wants to know if mere cohabitation is enough to establish a common-law marriage? Where is this topic discussed in the American Jurisprudence?

3. Your next door neighbor's dog is barking and keeping you up all night long. Where does the American Jurisprudence discuss dog barking being a nuisance? What NY case is cited as exempting dog barking as a nuisance?

4. Susan's son has just been qualified to enter into his school's gift and talented program. Susan wants you to find out more about public school's gifted programs. What Pennsylvania case, cited in the Corpus Juris Secundum (CJS), discusses mandatory gifted school programs to public school children?

5. In the CJS, what Texas case discusses the drug Dolophine?

6. What is the CJS definition of a pool table? What case is cited for the definition?

Series 2

1. After watching a stirring episode of "Law and Order: Traffic Safety Unit," you are inspired to find out what all this *Miranda* warning stuff is about. Cite the Corpus Juris Secundum article and American Jurisprudence sections that describe the warnings police are required to give to the newly arrested.

2. The SleepyTime Motel outside Lazy Eye, Nevada is home to a surprising assortment of drifters from all over the United States. Many of these folks are only passing through, but

they stop for the restaurant at the SleepyTime. The specialty dish is a honey cake with fresh coffee. The honey cake is made with real desert flower honey from the motel's own hives. These are located some 40 yards from the motel buildings, on a bluff overlooking a spectacular valley. Your client is Paul Oswald, a mucilage sales representative from Shoboshko, Wisconsin. He loves the smell of the desert in the morning and the honey cake has brought him to stay at the SleepyTime many times in the past. After a restful night, Paul decides to take in the sunrise over the valley before a fresh baked honey cake breakfast. If he had stopped for breakfast first he might have noticed the Lazy Eye Herald's cover story on the recent spate of livestock deaths due to an infestation of swarming killer bees. As it is, he is quietly standing on the bluff near the hives when a strange haze descends over the sun. Yes, Paul is one of the few people to see a squadron of killer bees in attack formation and live to tell the tale. Not realizing the gravity of the situation, Paul stares transfixed at the swirling mass of homicidal insects. Just in time, the spell is broken and Paul begins to sprint for the safety of the SleepyTime lobby. Paul is stung several dozen times before the motel maintenance personnel are able to spray him off with a hose. The SleepyTime management gives Paul a free night stay and a honey cake special, but he is still upset about his ordeal. What section of American Jurisprudence discusses a similar case? What case discusses a hotel guest bit by a rat?

3. Your old high school buddy Daryl has always had an exciting life. Daryl travels the world as a cameraman with SBNN (Sound Bite News Network). He got a special present from a group of survivalists in eastern Oklahoma, "So he'd be ready when the U.N. black helicopters descend upon the Americas." The gift is a chrome plated .45 caliber pistol. Unfortunately, Daryl was in such a hurry to get back into an urban area for a Frappucino and some sanity that he simply shoved the handgun under the seat of his car. Speeding along a two lane suburban road, Daryl is pulled over by a local police officer. Daryl is asked to submit to a search of the car and he consents, forgetting about the firearm under his seat. Daryl is released on bond after being arraigned for possession of a concealed weapon. He asks you to research this issue for him, and to tell him if Oklahoma has any exceptions to the law against possession of concealed weapons. Using only the Corpus Juris Secundum, answer the following questions: What section of the CJS discusses concealed weapons? Is there an exception apposite to these facts? Are there any Oklahoma cases cited in this section?

4. One day Cindy Davis comes into your office looking for representation. She is a master Saab mechanic. Her expertise makes her a valuable employee for many dealerships and repair shops. Ms. Davis is happy at her current job, but the shop owner chain smokes. Ms. Davis believes that the second hand smoke is harming her health. What Corpus Juris Secundum article discusses this issue? What American Jurisprudence section is the most relevant to this issue?

Treatise Exercises

Use the treatises indicated below to answer the following questions:

Series 1

Farnsworth on Contracts:

1. According to Farnsworth on Contracts, how can one terminate the power of acceptance?

2. What Illinois case, cited in Farnsworth on Contracts, explains further the idea of lapse of the offer?

Williston on Contracts:

3. What does Williston say is the difference between usage and custom?

4. What Massachusetts's case distinguished usage and custom?

Murray on Contracts:

5. What is the difference, according to Murray on Contracts, between an unilateral and a bilateral contract?

6. According to Murray on Contracts, what are the two tests of unconscionability?

Nimmer on Copyright:

7. What does Nimmer on Copyright say about the definition of "musical works" (altered)?

8. How does Nimmer define "derivative work" for copyright purposes?

Couch on Insurance 3d:

9. According to § 35:4 of Couch on Insurance, who may object to breach of Prohibitory

Clause?

10. What topic is covered in § 42:1 of Couch on Insurance? When does the husband have an insurable interest in his wife's property?

Restatement (Second) of Contracts:

1. According to Restatement (Second) of Contracts, what parties are required for the forming of a contract?

2. What topic is covered in Restatement (Second) of Contracts § 149? What happens when the second contract is unenforceable under the Statute of Frauds?

Restatement (Second) of Torts:

3. According to Restatement 2d on Torts, how can one commit conversion?

4. According to Restatement 2d on Torts, what are the minimum skills required of a dentist?

Restatement (Second) of Agency:

5. According to Restatement 2d on Agency, what is an escrow holder?

6. What is the liability, according to Restatement 2d on Agency, of an agent to another in assault?

Series 2

1. You are on a float trip down the Kokosing River in Ohio with a group of law students. One of your party trips over a rock and hurts his arm. Luckily, your mother forced you to join the "Young Explorers" when you were in grade school. You quickly convert a nearby sapling into a makeshift splint and, using vines, begin tying your fallen comrade's arm down, hopefully, setting the bone in the process. The other students are muttering something about liability and a roller skating rink case. Does the Second Restatement of Torts § 892D have any bearing on this problem?

2. Your cousin has negotiated a million-dollar deal to purchase a piece of real property commonly known as The Brooklyn Bridge, with an option to purchase the Lincoln Tunnel for a fixed price within two years thereafter. He wants to get out of the sale agreement. The agreement is completely oral. The sale is set to close in a few days. You ask around and you think that the statute of frauds could be useful for getting out of the contract. Since you don't have an expert understanding of the statute of frauds, you decide to consult a treatise, Corbin on Contracts. Which volume and section of Corbin on Contracts talks about the statute of frauds? How is the statute of frauds raised in litigation?

3. You are a Magistrate Judge in the Western District of Washington. You are presiding over a misdemeanor drug trial. There sits the accused, your childhood nemesis. Back in grade school Joseph Escargot was known as "Little Joey," and you find out that he still carries this nickname because it is listed as an alias on the indictment. He has diversified his criminal activities since starting out in the playground extortion field many years ago. You suppress a gleeful grin at the thought of presiding over his downfall, and are even happier to realize that Little Joey does not even recognize you. Because your internal ethics meter is making a loud racket, you decide to consult Moore's Federal Practice, just to check if there are any problems of bias in your presiding over this matter. Of what magnitude is the disqualification of a biased federal judge? What section answers this question?

4. Your friend, let's call him "Lobert" so as to disguise his real name, went down to Cancun with his (former) girlfriend for spring break last year. Lobert brought a disposable camera with him. During the trip much fun was had by all. After a wild evening at the cantina, Lobert took some rather risque' photographs of his girlfriend. After returning home, Lobert dropped the film off at Stuff-Mart for processing. When he received the prints, Lobert was surprised to find that some of the photos had been removed and replaced with a notice that Stuff-Mart has a strict policy against developing pictures unsuitable for family enjoyment. Lobert is disappointed but thinks nothing of it. Several weeks later he notices that his girlfriend is being stared at by an unusual number of people when they go out in public. Soon people are openly laughing at her, and she is even harassed in school. After the story came out, she transferred to another school at great expense and humiliation.[8] The couple broke up, and Lobert's girlfriend seeks a legal remedy against Stuff-Mart for invasion of privacy. Use Prosser and Keeton's torts treatise to answer the following questions: What section of the treatise discusses the tort doctrine of invasion of privacy? How many torts make up privacy doctrine? What action would be apposite to

---

[8] This is based on a real case. Lake v. Wal-Mart Stores, Inc., 582 N.W.2d 231 (Minn. 1998).

the above facts? What are the elements that Lobert's girlfriend will need to prove in order to prevail in her action against Stuff-Mart?

Law Reviews

Series 1

1. What is the title of the article cited 68 Mich. L. Rev. 389? Who wrote this article?

2. What page in volume 29 of the New England Law Review does the article, "Criminal Law's Greatest Mystery Thriller: Corporate Guilt Through Collective Knowledge" begin on?

3. What article is cited as 9 Ohio North. L. Rev. 369? Who is Marshall B. Kapp?

4. Who is the editor-in-chief of volume 33 of the University of Michigan Journal of Law Reform?

5. What article did Robert J. Rabin write in 30 Syracuse L. Rev.?

Use the Legal Periodicals Index to answer the next questions:

6. What law review article did Kevin Urick write in 1988?

7. How many articles did Jethro Busch write in 1999?

8. What law review article did Jesse Goldner write in 1993?

Series 2

Use the Index to Legal Periodicals, Shepard's, and the law reviews in your library to answer the following questions:

1. What Supreme Court cases are cited on page 399 of Volume 73 of the Michigan Law Review (just give the volume and page number from the reporter)?

2. What federal appellate case cited the article Breach of Confidence, 82 Colum. L. Rev. 1426?

3. Who wrote the 1997 Journal of Taxation article on the generation skipping transfer tax?

4. What article(s) did Adrian Hunt author in 1998?

5. What law review article did Jesse Goldner write in 1998? If there are more than one, give the first. Cite the article in Bluebook format.

Chapter 14
COURT RULES, LOCAL RULES, AND LOOSE-LEAF SERVICES

RESEARCH EXERCISES

Court Rules and Local Rules

1. What federal procedural rule governs the timeliness of an appeal?

2. What issue is addressed by the Federal District Court for the Northern District of Texas' local rule 53.1?

3. On what days is the U.S. District Court for the District of Utah open until 5:00pm?

Loose Leaf Services

4. BNA's Health Law & Business, loose-leaf series contains a sample confidentiality agreement. What is the page number for this agreement? What is the first word of the second numbered paragraph of that agreement?

5. What paragraph number is medical service contract depreciation indexed under in CCH's Standard Federal Tax Reporter series for the year 2005? What page number is that paragraph number on?

Chapter 15
CONSTITUTIONS AND FEDERAL, STATE, AND MUNICIPAL LEGISLATION

RESEARCH EXERCISES

1. Where do you find the official, "proof positive" version of U.S. laws that have not been codified and reenacted? Where is the office text of the laws that have been codified and reenacted?

2. Find 63 Stat. 1166. Is this a public or a private law? What is the proper citation to this law? What happened to Eiko Nakamura?

3. When was P.L.103-322 passed?

4. What effect did Public Law 103-322 § 330016 have on United States Code, Title 18?

5. What was the penalty for counterfeiting under 1 Stat. 115 § 14?

6. In what volumes of the U.S.C.A. do you find the Constitution of the United States of America? What case is cited in a subsection dealing with obscenity and sunbathing?

7. Your client accidentally set an American flag on fire at a Fourth of July parade. Several law enforcement officials witnessed the event and took down his name, address and telephone number. Client fears that he may be subject to a fine or other penalty for desecration or destruction of the flag. Using the General Index to the United States Code Annotated (soft cover volumes), see if you can find entries for desecration of the flag and for penalties associated therewith. What headings and subheadings of the index do you find, and what sections of the code are you referred to? Does one of those sections concern respect for the flag?

8. Under the section(s) of the code found above, is it considered properly respectful of the flag to use it as bedding or drapery in your home, especially if you festoon the flag in the

process? What is the public law number of the act that created this section, and what is the date of enactment? Referring to the provision on fines and penalties that you found above, what is the criminal penalty (maximum fine or prison time) for desecration of the flag?

9. Your client has seen a rhinoceros tusk offered for sale on eBay. Client has recently learned that rhinoceros are endangered species, and she wonders if there are laws concerning the handling of rhinoceros parts. Using the General Index to the United States Code Annotated, is there a section (or a string of sections) of the United States Code concerning rhinoceros conservation? (Give the index heading and subheading and the code section(s)). What is the name of this title of the United States Code?

10. In section 1540(b) of the title of the United States Code found in response to question 9 above, what is the criminal penalty (maximum fine or prison time) for knowing violations of that chapter? What subsection to section 1540 of this title has recently been added (as indicated by the pocket part to this section)? Give the letter and title of the subsection.

Chapter 16
LEGISLATIVE HISTORY

RESEARCH EXERCISES:

Federal Legislative History

1. Your firm represents Teluwhat!™, a consortium of startup telecommunications companies scattered throughout the United States. The member companies' operations center primarily on the provision of low cost telephone and datacom service for small businesses and residential/consumer markets. Most of the member companies have been formed in the past two years. They are very concerned about the impact of FBI wiretapping requirements on their business. Multiple law enforcement wiretap requests have been coming to the consortium members every day. It is requiring a large investment of time and money to satisfy all of these requests. The FBI claims that they have the right to ask for these lawful requests whenever they want under 47 U.S.C. § 1001. The partner for whom you work has asked you to compile a legislative history on this law. Answer the following questions about this legislation:

   What is the short title of this legislation? What is its public law number? What was its original bill number?

2. Obtain a copy of the CIS/INDEX legislative history abstract for this bill. In the summary, what provisions did the house report recommend be added to the bill with regard to cellular phone service?

3. Did the listed Report(s) recommend passage of the bill?

4. What **House** Report(s) were prepared on this legislation during the 103rd Congress?

Using Westlaw, find and print a copy of the House Report(s) listed in your answer to question 4. Use the printout(s) to answer the following questions:

5. How many hearings were held during the 103rd Congress about this legislation? What were the dates of those hearings? Which committees were the hearings held before?

6. Who is (was) Roy Neel? What does RBOC stand for?

7. What was the major problem that the legislation was designed to remedy?

8. According to the report(s), was it Congress' intent to have this legislation cover the activities of Internet Service Providers?

Locate and view a copy of Louis J. Freeh's, March 18, 1994 testimony to Congress using Westlaw. You do not need to print this document. Answer the following question using only the first paragraph:

9. What does Mr. Freeh identify as the source of a major threat to effective law enforcement?

Chapter 17
FEDERAL REGULATORY AND ADMINISTRATIVE LAW

RESEARCH EXERCISES

The Code of Federal Regulations

Your firm's biggest client is Acme Medical Assoc. ("AMA"), a clinical medical testing firm. AMA president Clara Beaker would like to know how the federal government defines a nephelometer. Answer the following questions using ONLY the Code of Federal Regulations, LSA pamphlets, and the Federal Register.

1. What C.F.R. part discusses clinical chemistry and toxicology devices?

2. What C.F.R. subpart defines a "nephelometer"? What subpart classifies it?

3. Has this regulation been updated during the year 2000?

Answer the following questions ONLY if you found that the regulation has been updated in the year 2000.

4. Where was it updated in the Federal Register?

5. What did the update consist of?

Chapter 19
STRATEGIES FOR RESEARCH AND DETERMINING WHEN YOU ARE FINISHED

RESEARCH REVIEW

1. Explain two reasons why you might use *Shepard's Citations* in the course of researching a legal issue.

2. Explain the difference between primary sources and secondary sources. List one example of each type of source.

3. Explain two benefits of using the United States Code Annotated instead of the United States Code to conduct federal statutory research.

4. Explain why you would not quote a headnote from a case in an office memorandum.

5. Write a case citation using correct Bluebook form based on the following information: Paula Corbin Jones, Plaintiff, sued William Jefferson Clinton, Defendant. This case was decided by the United States Court of Appeals for the Fourth Circuit on July 29, 1999. It appears in volume 159, page 821, of the Federal Reporter, Third Series.

6. List all of the possible reporters in which you might find a case decided by the Supreme Court of Illinois.

Chapter 22
MOTIONS TO DISMISS

WRITING EXERCISES

Exercise 1. Consider the following set of facts:

MEMORANDUM

TO: Junior Associate

FROM: Senior Partner

DATE: January 18, 2000

RE: Jiang v. Piao-Liang

SUBJECT: Motion to Dismiss for Lack of Jurisdiction

Patricia Piao-Liang Davis is a 20 year old super-model who goes by the professional name "Piao-Liang." She was born in Nanjing, PRC in 1979, but was orphaned at four months of age, and was adopted at six months of age by Clifford and June Davis, U.S. citizens, and raised in Provo, Utah. Piao-Liang is a naturalized citizen of the United States, and is domiciled and resident in Provo, Utah. Piao-Liang has joined a group of other super-models who offer their unfertilized ova for auction on an internet site known as Dezyner-Genes.com. Although she has participated in the web site since January 1999, she has never accepted any bids to purchase her eggs.

While on a photo-shoot for Drop Dead Gorgeous magazine that took her to various locations in China (the Great Wall and Tiananmen Square in Beijing, the Bund in Shanghai, and others), Piao-Liang was approached at West Lake in Hangzhou by a businessman, Mr. Jiang "Jerry" Chuang-ping. Mr. Jiang explained that his wife was infertile, and he was interested in purchasing an ovum from Piao-Liang, and offered her $1 million for it. She was flattered and orally agreed to the transaction. The two drank baijiu and toasted each other several times to celebrate the deal. When she returned to the United States, Piao-Liang's lawyers, Dott, Tee & Crosseye, reviewed Mr. Jiang's written proposal for the agreement concerning the sale of the ovum, and they accepted the terms, but added a forum selection and choice of law clause in the agreement, specifying that any action arising under the contract would be brought in a state or federal court in Utah and that the law of Utah would govern the contract. The contract was signed by Piao-Liang in New York, NY, on November 2, 1999, and by Mr. Jiang in Taibei, Republic of China (Taiwan), on November 4, 1999. The egg or eggs were to be delivered by June 1, 2000, and the payment of $1 million was to be made immediately upon successful fertilization and implantation.

Jerry Jiang, age 49, is a naturalized American citizen who owns a controlling interest in and supervises four factories producing computer memory chips in Taibei. He was born in Taibei in 1950. He immigrated to the United States in 1979, and was naturalized as a U.S. citizen in 1984. Although he first settled in San Francisco, he now lives and works seven months of the year in Taiwan, and owns a condominium in Taibei. The rest of the year he travels or stays at one of his two homes in San Francisco, California and Aspen, Colorado. His wife, Sun Li, travels with him and stays wherever he is staying throughout the year. (The couple have no children and cannot have any because Sun Li is infertile.) Jiang and Sun have followed this routine every year for the last twelve years, but Jiang has made it known that he intends to retire to Taiwan when he turns 60. He has a California driver's license and a U.S. Passport, but he is still recognized by the government of the Republic of China as having dual-citizenship, and also has a Republic of China passport. He votes, registers his car, and pays taxes in California, but he also pays taxes in Taiwan. He owns a distribution warehouse in Salt Lake City, UT, and does an average of $200,000 in Utah each year.

Piao-Liang discovered in late November that Mr. Jiang is the nephew of the late General and President of the ROC, Jiang Ji-shi, better known to the world as Chiang Kai-shek. This horrified her, since her Chinese family had been oppressed by the Nationalists prior to the Communist victory in China. She decided to refuse to go through with the sale, and Mr. Jiang sued her in the United States District Court for the District of Utah.

Piao-Liang has filed a motion to dismiss for lack of subject matter jurisdiction. Please prepare a memorandum to support our position in this matter. Further information accompanies this memorandum.

UNITED STATES DISTRICT COURT
DISTRICT OF UTAH
CENTRAL DIVISION

JIANG CHUANG-PING,	)	
	)	
Plaintiff,	)	No. 2:99-CV-2345-K
	)	(Judge Kimball)
	)	
PATRICIA PIAO-LIANG DAVIS, A/K/A	)	JURY TRIAL DEMANDED
"PIAO-LIANG",	)	
	)	
Defendant.	)	

COMPLAINT

NOW COMES Plaintiff Jiang Chuang-ping ("Plaintiff"), and for his complaint against Defendant Patricia Piao-Liang Davis, also known as the supermodel "Piao-Liang ("Defendant"), states as follows:

PARTIES

1. Plaintiff is a citizen and resident of the City of San Francisco, State of California, and the United States of America. He is domiciled in the State of California.

2. Defendant Piao-Liang is a citizen and resident of the State of Utah, United States of America, and is domiciled in Provo, Utah, in this District.

JURISDICTION AND VENUE

3. This Court has subject matter jurisdiction over this action under 28 U.S.C. § 1332(a)(1) in that Plaintiff and Defendant have diverse citizenship, and the matter involves over $75,000 in controversy.

4. Personal jurisdiction exists over Defendant because Defendant is a citizen and resident of the State of Utah and of this District and Division and is subject to service of process in this State and District.

5. Defendant and Plaintiff entered into the Contract attached hereto as Exhibit 1 ("Contract") on November 2 and November 4, 1999, respectively.

6. The contract provides for suit to be brought in a federal court in Utah and the Contract is to be governed by Utah law. Contract, section 5.

7. Venue is proper in this district pursuant to the forum selection clause in section 5 of the Contract and pursuant to 28 U.S.C. § 1391(a)(1),(2), in that Defendant is resident and domiciled in this District and Division, and the subject matter of the Contract is present in this District.

COUNT I - BREACH OF CONTRACT

8. On November 2, 1999, Defendant entered into the Contract, promising to deliver to Plaintiff's OB-GYN physician one or more healthy and viable ova from her ovaries at the first available opportunity and no later than June 1, 2000. Upon receipt and successful fertilization and implantation of the egg(s) in Plaintiff's wife's uterus, Plaintiff was to pay Plaintiff by wire transfer the sum of one million United States dollars.

9. On December 18, 1999, Defendant phoned Plaintiff and repudiated the contract by stating that she would not perform her obligations. She then, on that same day, sent by facsimile transmission and U.S. Mail the letter attached hereto as Exhibit 2, again repudiating the Contract and refusing to perform her obligations under the Contract.

10. Plaintiff was and remains ready to perform his obligations under the Contract, and there are no other conditions precedent to the agreement that would prevent its performance.

11. Defendant breached its agreement with Plaintiff by anticipatory repudiation.

12. Plaintiff has no available alternative remedy at law that could replace or compensate Plaintiff for the unique value of the subject matter of the Contract, and seeks specific performance of the Contract, and such further and other relief as the Court deems proper in the circumstances.

COUNT II - SPECIFIC PERFORMANCE

13. Plaintiff realleges the allegations of paragraphs 1-12 of this complaint as though set forth fully in this paragraph.

14. Plaintiff comes to this court seeking equity, with clean hands, and with the equities in his favor. Plaintiff has no available alternative remedy at law. The public policy of this jurisdiction favors the upholding and enforcement of contracts for the provision of a unique subject matter.

15. Defendant has repudiated and breached her obligations under the Contract. The equities and public policy are against Defendant.

16. Plaintiff seeks specific performance of the Contract.

WHEREFORE, Plaintiff requests the Court to order Defendant to deliver to Plaintiff's OB-GYN physician one or more healthy and viable ova from her ovaries at the first available opportunity and no later than June 1, 2000, and to award Plaintiff such further and other relief as the Court deems proper in the circumstances.

JURY TRIAL DEMANDED.

FINLEY, KRUMBLE & BREAKUP, LLP

By:____________________________________

Miriam O. McGuinnis Ut Bar No. 02112
Thor X. Wang Ut Bar No. 04523
Xavier Rocque de Hassad Ut Bar No. 16753
114 Market Street, Suite 2800
Salt Lake City, Utah 84101
Phone: 801-555-SU4U
Fax: 801-555-PAYU

Attorneys for Plaintiff Jiang Chuang-ping

Purchase and Sale Contract

WHEREFORE, Mr. Jerry Jiang Chuang-Ping (Buyer) and Ms. Patricia Piao-Liang Davis (Seller) wish to enter into an agreement for the transfer of at least one egg from Seller's ovaries to Buyer for the purpose of fertilization of the egg and implantation in Buyer's wife; and

WHEREFORE, the parties, Buyer and Seller, in consideration of the mutual promises stated herein and for other good and valuable consideration; and

WHEREFORE, the parties, Buyer and Seller, wish to complete this transaction at the earliest practicable time, and in no event later than June 1, 2000;

Then the parties covenant and agree to the following:

1. At the earliest practicable opportunity, and in no event later than June 1, 2000, in New York City, NY or Salt Lake City, UT, or at any other mutually agreeable location, Seller shall deliver to Buyer's OB-GYN physician one or more healthy and viable ova (i.e., eggs) from her ovaries.

2. Upon receipt and successful fertilization of the egg(s), the egg(s) are to be implanted in Buyer's wife's uterus.

3. After successful implantation of the fertilized egg(s) in Buyer's wife's uterus, without miscarriage, for twenty-one days, Buyer shall pay Seller by wire transfer to Osmond National Bank, Account No. 100223456 owned by Seller, the sum of one million United States dollars.

4. In the event that conditions 2 and 3 cannot be successfully completed with the initial supply of the egg(s) from Seller, Seller shall, within six weeks of notification by facsimile or U.S. mail by Buyer of the failure of conditions 2 or 3, supply one or more additional healthy and viable eggs to Buyer's OB-GYN physician in New York City, NY or Salt Lake City, UT, and shall continue to supply eggs in the manner described in this paragraph every six weeks until successful completion of conditions 2 and 3 of this contract.

5. Should any dispute between the parties arise under this agreement, the parties, Buyer and Seller, agree that all disputes shall be resolved in litigation that shall be filed in a state or federal court in the State of Utah and all conditions and terms and obligations of this contract shall be governed by and interpreted under Utah law.

Signed by Buyer:

____

Jerry Jiang Chuang-ping
Date: November ____, 1999

Signed by Seller:

____

Patricia Piao-Liang Davis
Date: November _____, 1999

Exhibit 1

Piao-Liang® is Beauty
234 Joseph Smith Drive
Provo, UT 84602 USA
(801) 555-piao

December 18, 1999

By Facsimile and Mail:

Mr. Jerry "Nationalist Liar" Jiang Chuang-ping
Two Embarcadero Center, Suite 3801
San Francisco, CA 94111-3909
Phone: 415-555-7779
Fax: 888-555-7789

Pay attention to this:

You can forget the deal, you Nationalist Pig. I will never go through with it with YOU and your barren wife. Pi hua! Good luck tricking some other Zhongguo Nu Haizi to give up her eggs to you. You will NEVER get one of my eggs so that you can perpetuate your murderous line.

I wish you a nice flat road on your journey -- as flat as your wife's ovaries! (HA!)
Zai-jian Guomindang Puppet Boy.

Sincerely,

Piao-Liang

Exhibit 2

UNITED STATES DISTRICT COURT
DISTRICT OF UTAH
CENTRAL DIVISION

JIANG CHUANG-PING, Plaintiff,	)	No. 2:99-CV-2345-K
v.	)	
PATRICIA PIAO-LIANG DAVIS, Defendant.	)	

MOTION TO DISMISS

NOW COMES defendant Patricia Piao-Liang Davis ("Piao-Liang"), and moves this Court pursuant to Fed. R. Civ. P. 12(b)(1), to dismiss this action for lack of subject matter jurisdiction.

Plaintiff seeks this Court to take jurisdiction over the subject matter of this action under 28 U.S.C. § 1332(a)(1), alleging diversity of citizenship of the parties and a proper jurisdictional amount. As will be discussed in more detail in the Defendant's Memorandum in Support of the Motion to Dismiss, to be filed on February 14, 2000, the first requirement, diversity, cannot be met by Plaintiff, because Plaintiff is not a citizen or resident of any State of the United States, and does not possess diverse citizenship within the meaning of 28 U.S.C. § 1332(a)(1). In that Plaintiff is not a citizen and resident of any state of the United States for diversity purposes, this fact defeats the assertion of diversity jurisdiction over the subject matter of this action, and the action must be dismissed.

WHEREFORE, Defendant Piao-Liang prays the Court dismiss this action and award Defendant costs and expenses and such further and other relief as the Court deems appropriate in this matter.

Respectfully Submitted,
DOTT, TEE & CROSSEYE P.C.

By:________________________________

Attorneys admitted *pro hac vice*
by Order of Court dated 1/6/2000

Sandra Glib Gabber Mo. Bar No. 41044
Marvin T. Bosley Mo. Bar No. 45234
Marta Graham Park Mo. Bar No. 65239
1010 Walnut Street, Suite 200
St. Louis, Missouri 63101
Phone: (314) 555-9900
Fax: (314) 555-9901
Attorneys for Defendant Patricia Piao-Liang Davis

UNITED STATES DISTRICT COURT
DISTRICT OF UTAH
CENTRAL DIVISION

JIANG CHUANG-PING,	)	
	)	
Plaintiff,	)	No. 2:99-CV-2345-K
v.	)	
	)	
PATRICIA PIAO-LIANG DAVIS,	)	
	)	
Defendant.	)	

DECLARATION OF JERRY JIANG CHUANG-PING

I, Jiang "Jerry" Chuang-ping , of lawful age, do swear under penalty of perjury of the laws of the United States and the State of Utah that I have first hand information concerning the following and the following information is true and correct:

1. I am 42 years old. I am a naturalized United States citizen, and I reside in San Francisco, CA.

2. I am the president and CEO of Jiang Memory Solutions, Ltd., a corporation that has production and distribution facilities in San Jose, CA, Salt Lake City, UT, Redmond, WA, Festus, MO, and Taibei, Republic of China. I supervise four factories producing computer memory chips in Taibei, and the distribution facilities in the United States. Because of these responsibilities, I travel a great deal and am outside the United States on business and for recreation for months at a time. It is common for my business to require me to spend seven or more months outside the United States each year.

3. I have considered California to be my and my wife's home since we immigrated there in 1979. I have no desire to settle in any other state of the United States. My wife and I plan to stay in California for the indefinite future. I have a United States passport and a California driver's license. I have owned a house at 231 Cobb Hill Drive in San Francisco for eleven years, and have leased office space at Two Embarcadero Center, Suite 3801, San Francisco, CA 94111-3909, for seven years. I am registered to vote in California. I have paid taxes to the City and County of San Francisco, the State of California, and the United States from 1979 to the present. I own three vehicles registered in California.

4. I have four bank accounts at BankofAmerica in San Francisco and two bank accounts at BankofAmerica, New York. I also have one account at IBJ Schroeder in Tokyo, Japan, and four accounts at Guomin Bank, Taibei, Republic of China. My checking and

commercial line of credit account at BankofAmerica, New York is the largest account I own measured by amount of deposit.

FURTHER DECLARANT SAYETH NAUGHT.

Sworn to under penalty of perjury on this 29th day of December 1999.

____

Jerry Jiang Chuang-ping

UNITED STATES DISTRICT COURT
DISTRICT OF UTAH
CENTRAL DIVISION

JIANG CHUANG-PING,	)	
	)	
Plaintiff,	)	No. 2:99-CV-2345-K
v.	)	
	)	
PATRICIA PIAO-LIANG DAVIS,	)	
	)	
Defendant.	)	

DECLARATION OF CHAIM ESCOBAR

I, Chaim Escobar, of lawful age, do swear under penalty of perjury of the laws of the United States and the State of Utah that I have first hand information concerning the following and the following information is true and correct:

1. I am 39 years old. I am the owner and operator of Chaim's Search and Serve, a private investigatory service in San Francisco, CA.

2. I have personally investigated and obtained the following information about Mr. Jiang Chuang-ping, a/k/a Jerry Jiang, the plaintiff in the above captioned matter.

3. Jerry Jiang was born in Taibei, Taiwan in 1950. He immigrated to the United States in 1979, and was naturalized as a U.S. citizen in 1984.

4. Jiang owns a controlling interest in and supervises four factories producing computer memory chips in Taibei. These factories are his primary source of employment and income.

5. Although he first settled in San Francisco, he now lives and works seven months of the year in Taiwan, and owns a condominium in Taibei. The rest of the year he travels or stays at one of the two homes he owns in San Francisco, California and Aspen, Colorado. His wife, Sun Li, travels with him and stays wherever he is staying throughout the year.

6. Jiang and Sun have followed this routine of living seven or more months in Taiwan every year for the last twelve years.

7. Through interviews with his neighbors, Cliff Zhang and Will Xu, and employees Rajin Sihgn, Kali Patel, and Charlie Wu at his San Jose plant, I have learned that Jiang regularly

states that he intends to retire to Taiwan when he turns 60.

8. Jiang has a California driver's license and a U.S. Passport, but he is recognized by the government of the Republic of China as having dual-citizenship, and also has a Republic of China passport. He uses the Republic of China passport on trips throughout Asia, but never when he flies back and forth to the United States.

9. Jiang has four bank accounts in Taibei, Taiwan at the Guomin Bank (National Bank of Taiwan). He has other accounts across the globe in Tokyo, New York, and San Francisco, but his two most active accounts in terms of number of deposits, wire transfers, checks drawn, and other transactions are both at Guomin Bank in Taiwan. He has paid corporate income taxes and personal income taxes and property taxes to Taiwan every year since 1970 (the earliest year such records are available).

FURTHER DECLARANT SAYETH NAUGHT.

Sworn to under penalty of perjury on this 9th day of January, 2000.

____

Mr. Chaim Escobar

BACKGROUND PRINCIPLES OF LAW

(Note: This is not a legal brief or memorandum in support of a motion. It is not in the proper form of an argument section. Do not view it as a sample or model of good argument)

A. DAVIS'S ARGUMENT THAT THERE IS NO DIVERSITY JURISDICTION UNDER 1332(a)(1).

The court must determine someone's domicile using a variety of factors. Coury v. Prot, 85 F.3d 244, 250 (5th Cir 1996). Davis will argue that because Jiang has established domicile in China and is a U.S. citizen, he no longer may bring a diversity action under § 1332. See Sadat v. Mertes, 615 F.2d 1176, 1180 (7th Cir. 1980); General Electric v. Cugini, 640 F. Supp. 113, 115 (D. Puerto Rico 1986).

In general, the motion to dismiss must argue that Jiang has expressed an intent to create a new domicile and has acted to carry that intent into effect. See Johnston v. Cordell, 421 F.2d 1310, 1312 (10th Cir. 1970) (*citing* Mid-Continent Pipe Line Co. v. Whiteley, 116 F.2d 871 (10th Cir. 1941). That is, Jiang has express his intent to return to China permanently at age 60 and establish domicile there. He has also acted to carry that intent into effect by moving there seven months out of the year. Davis's would argue the mere holding of a driver's license and voter registration and owns some property may not be enough to establish domicile in California. He pays taxes wherever he lives and does business — that is not a determinative factor. Also she would focus on the fact that he had property in a foreign state, carries a passport from that state, and made it known that his intent was to retire to a foreign state.

B. JERRY'S ARGUMENT THAT THERE IS DIVERSITY JURISDICTION UNDER 1332(a)(1).

Jiang, the plaintiff, must argue that he established domicile in San Francisco, California, and has maintained that status. Once a domicile is established, it is presumed to remain the domicile of the person until there is a change. See Lilley v. Dunnavent, No. 99-1023-JTM, 1999 WL 1096037, *2 (D. Kan. Nov. 23, 1999) (citing Lew v. Moss, 797 F.2d 747, 751 (9th Cir. 1986)); Maple Island Farm v. Bitterling, 196 F.2d 55 (8th Cir. 1952). He must argue that Piao-Liang has not established enough evidence to rebut that presumption.

In addition, Jiang will also assert that objective indicia are often looked at to establish one's domicile. One's mere "mental fixings" are not enough to change domicile. D.H. Walden Co. v. Broce Constr. Co., 357 F.2d 242, 245 (10th Cir. 1966). Thus, Jiang can point to his California residence, his California driver's license, his San Francisco headquarters, his voter registration, his U.S. Passport, and his paying of taxes. While he is living in China part of the year, he always returns to California and does not intend to change domicile until the age of 60 — ten years from now. Thus, he only has a "floating intention" to end his California citizenship upon retirement. See Gates v. Commissioner, 199 F.2d 291, 294 (10th Cir. 1952); see also Cugini, 640 F. Supp. at 115.

A person's domicile persists until a new one is acquired or clearly abandoned. Gates, 199 F.2d at 294; see also Cugini, 640 F. Supp. at 115. An intention to live permanently at the claimed domicile is not required. Holmes v. Sopuch, 639 F.2d 431 (8th Cir. 1981). Jerry's best argument should be that his intention to move in the future did not establish his present domicile and also focus on his presence in foreign jurisdictions purely as a result of business demands.

---

1. Using the above fact pattern and complaint, draft an Introduction section for **defendant's** motion to dismiss on the basis of lack of personal jurisdiction.

2. Using the above fact pattern and complaint, draft a Statement of Facts section for **defendant's** motion to dismiss on the basis of lack of personal jurisdiction.

3. Draft 3-5 paragraphs of the Argument section of **defendant's** motion to dismiss on the basis of lack of personal jurisdiction. Make use of the cases cited in the Background Principles of Law section above.

4. Assume that you represent the plaintiff. Using the above fact pattern and complaint, draft an Introduction section for **plaintiff's** opposition to defendant's motion to dismiss on the basis of lack of personal jurisdiction.

5. Using the above fact pattern and complaint, draft a Statement of Facts section for **plaintiff's** opposition to defendant's motion to dismiss on the basis of lack of personal jurisdiction.

6. Draft 3-5 paragraphs of the Argument section of **plaintiff's** opposition to defendant's motion to dismiss on the basis of lack of personal jurisdiction. Make use of the cases cited in the Background Principles of Law section above.

Exercise 2. Consider the following set of facts:

MEMORANDUM

TO: [Your name]

FROM: Glib Gabber, Chairman of the Commercial Litigation Group

DATE: January 19, 1999

Our client, Trans-Urban Resource Directories, has been sued in the United States District Court for the Eastern District of Missouri (*see* attached complaint). Trans-Urban creates software for computer networks that scans the hard drives of stand-alone computers linked into a local area network and collects and compiles information about the files on these stand-alone computers, and then creates graphical directories of the contents using a web page interface, so that organizations using the software can turn their local area network into a kind of "intranet." People linked into the network can retrieve, review, and edit documents and projects simultaneously, and have access to the collective information of the company even if it is found on certain persons' hard-drives. (Privacy is protected because individual users can maintain private, password-protected folders on their hard drives where non-work related material can be stored.) The software is called "Lan2Net" version 1.01.

Trans-Urban is a four-man operation. It is based in Anchorage, Alaska, and all of it's personnel and everything associated with its business (all files, computers, records, equipment, and "copies" of the software) are located in Anchorage. Trans-Urban maintains a website on the World Wide Web, at URL www.lan2net.com, which advertises and provides information about the Lan2Net software. The site and all of its files are hosted by an internet service provider in Anchorage, Alaska, called "FishhookOnLine." At the Lan2Net website, a visitor can read about the product and its features, click a mailto: link and send email to Mr. Clifford Chance of Trans-Urban to ask questions about the product (Chance is one of the four owners of the company, a vice-president, and the director of technical services), and actually order the product by filling out an on-line order form, giving a credit card number, and submitting the form. The submitted form is transmitted by email to Trans-Urban, who verifies the credit card before accepting the order. Then a confirmation of the accepted order is sent by email to the customer. In the confirmation email, the customer is given a special URL address to the download web page and is also given a password that enables them to download the software. The download page and all of its files are on the FishhookOnLine server in Anchorage.

The plaintiff in this action, Saint Mary's Entrepreneur Liquidation Loan Service, is a Missouri corporation, with all of its operations and personnel located in St. Louis, Missouri. St. Mary's wanted to buy some networking/intranet software, and found the Lan2Net website. St. Mary's sent an email to Clifford Chance asking if the Lan2Net software was Y2K compliant. Chance emailed back to St. Mary's a three word reply: "We think so." St. Mary's proceeded through the order process on the website, checked the license and warranty box to indicate "I accept these terms," and filled out an order for the software. Trans-Urban processed the order, and after verifying the credit card used, sent a confirmation of the sale with the download address and a password. St. Mary's apparently downloaded and installed the software, ran a check to see if the software was Y2K compliant (they changed the date on all of their system servers to December 31, 1999, and let the computers roll over to the year 2000), and crash! The whole thing apparently locked up. A big mess. They were shut down for two days getting some technicians in to repair the system, and they allegedly suffered some actual costs (of the repair) and collateral damage (lost profits, business interruption, a few corrupted files, etc.). Naturally, they sued Trans-Urban for their damages under two legal theories — breach of contract, and breach of the implied covenants of merchantability and fitness for a particular purpose under the Uniform Commercial Code.

Our first order of business is trying to get this complaint dismissed. I want you to draft a motion to dismiss based on the fact that Trans-Urban does not have sufficient contacts and connections with Missouri under the Missouri Long-Arm Statute and the U.S. Constitution's "due process/minimum contacts" standards. As indicated above, all contacts that Trans-Urban had with this customer are internet-related. The customer made the initial contact, asked their question through an email, and placed their order. Trans-Urban did send those two emails to St. Mary's in Missouri. They have no other customers in Missouri and are doing no other business or advertising in Missouri other than the fact that their website can be accessed in Missouri. Since the Lan2Net site was first published in August 1998, the site has received 123 visits from "persons" in Missouri, but St. Mary's was the only one to make an email inquiry and to order the product. No person associated with Trans-Urban has ever stepped foot in Missouri. The St. Mary's order was not accepted and completed until the credit card was approved and the order processed, all of which occurred in Anchorage, Alaska. Nothing was ever shipped into Missouri, because the customer had to download the software from a web page hosted by a server in Anchorage.

As you know, we are in federal court in Missouri, so the Eighth Circuit and U.S. Supreme Court govern this procedural issue of jurisdiction, although I expect we'll need to see how Missouri courts have interpreted their Long Arm Statute with regard to internet contacts, and we probably will need to look outside Missouri and the Eighth Circuit for cases involving the internet and personal jurisdiction. I don't want to touch the venue issue or *forum non coveniens* right now, so don't discuss these in your motion. Let's just draft a regular motion to dismiss for lack of personal jurisdiction.

UNITED STATES DISTRICT COURT
EASTERN DISTRICT OF MISSOURI
EASTERN DIVISION

ST. MARY'S ENTREPRENEUR LIQUIDATION LOAN SERVICE,	)	
Plaintiff,	)	
v.	)	No. 4:98-CV-9876-DJS
TRANS-URBAN RESOURCE DIRECTORIES,	)	JURY TRIAL DEMANDED
Defendant.	)	

COMPLAINT

Now comes plaintiff, St. Mary's Entrepreneur Liquidation Loan Service, and for its complaint against defendant Trans-Urban Resource Directories, states as follows:

PARTIES

1. Plaintiff St. Mary's Entrepreneur Liquidation Loan Service ("Plaintiff") is a Missouri Corporation with its principal place of business in the City of St. Louis, Missouri. At all relevant times, Plaintiff was authorized to conduct business in the State of Missouri, and maintained an office in the City of St. Louis, Missouri.

2. Defendant Trans-Urban Resource Directories ("Defendant") is an Alaska Corporation with its principal place of business in Anchorage, Alaska.

JURISDICTION AND VENUE

3. This Court has subject matter jurisdiction over this action under 28 U.S.C. § 1332 in that Plaintiff and Defendant have diverse citizenship, and the matter involves over $75,000 in controversy.

4. Personal jurisdiction exists over Defendant because Defendant has conducted business in the State of Missouri by advertising its products on the Internet and World Wide Web in Missouri, and by selling products in Missouri through its web site, http://www.lan2net.com ("Lan2Net Site"), which is accessible in Missouri. Furthermore, Defendant has made a contract in Missouri with a Missouri resident, Plaintiff. This action arises out of Defendant's doing business in Missouri and making a contract in Missouri, which satisfies two prongs under the Missouri Long-Arm Statute, Mo. Rev. Stat. § 506.500(1)(1),(2).

5. Venue is proper in this district pursuant to 28 U.S.C. § 1391(a)(1)-(3), (c), in that a substantial part of the events and occurrences from which this case arises occurred in St. Louis in the Eastern District of Missouri, and Defendant is subject to personal jurisdiction in the Eastern District of Missouri and therefore resides in this district.

COUNT I - BREACH OF CONTRACT

6. On November 10, 11, and 14, 1998, Plaintiff, in St. Louis, Missouri, accessed the Lan2Net Site to investigate a possible purchase of networking software. Defendant was advertising it's Lan2Net version 1.01 software product on this web site. Defendant's advertising explained that the software could convert a standard local area network ("LAN system") into an intranet for better collaboration and file-sharing between networked users. Defendant's product appeared to be just what Plaintiff was looking for.

7. Plaintiff was very concerned about the "millennium bug," and communicated by email with Defendant to ask if the Lan2Net software was "Y2K compliant" — a term of art in the computer industry that means that the software would not itself have any problems or dysfunction and would not cause any problems or dysfunction in connected computer systems at the turn of the century from December 31, 1999 to January 1, 2000. Defendant sent an email to Plaintiff in St. Louis, Missouri, stating unequivocally that they believed Lan2Net was Y2K compliant.

8. In reliance on this assurance from Defendant and on the advertising Defendant had put forth in Missouri on the Internet, on November 15, 1998, plaintiff placed an order with defendant and purchased four installation licenses of the Lan2Net software. Plaintiff never had to leave Missouri to get the software — it downloaded the software from an Internet web page accessible in St. Louis, Missouri.

9. Plaintiff installed the Lan2Net software on its computer system on November 17, 1998, and on November 18, 1998, Plaintiff tested the software by simulating a turn of the century transition. Plaintiff changed the internal timing clocks of all of their servers to December 31, 1999, and let the servers rollover into the year 2000. This type of test had been performed several times before to test the Y2K compliance of components of and the entirety of Plaintiff's computer system, and no errors or dysfunction had ever been experienced. However, after installation of the Lan2Net software, the turn of the century simulation revealed that the Lan2Net software was not Y2K compliant, and the Lan2Net software failed, causing Plaintiff's network to crash and lock up, tying up all of Plaintiff's business records, files, and work-in-progress for two full business days on November 18 and 19, 1998.

10. Plaintiff processes thousands of loan requests on a day to day basis, and maintains a portfolio of tens of thousands of customers. The interruption of plaintiff's business caused it to lose business and profits from approximately 1,500 new customers, as well as certain vital customer records, and directly resulted in the loss of thirteen existing customers and the profits from that business. The damages directly caused by Defendant's interruption of Plaintiff's

3. Draft 3-5 paragraphs of the Argument section of **defendant's** motion to dismiss on the basis of lack of diversity jurisdiction. Make use of the cases cited in the Background Principles of Law section above.

4. Assume that you represent the **plaintiff**. Using the above fact pattern and complaint, draft an Introduction section for **plaintiff's** opposition to defendant's motion to dismiss on the basis of lack of diversity jurisdiction.

5. Using the above fact pattern and complaint, draft a Statement of Facts section for **plaintiff's** opposition to defendant's motion to dismiss on the basis of lack of diversity jurisdiction.

6. Draft 3-5 paragraphs of the Argument section of **plaintiff's** opposition to defendant's motion to dismiss on the basis of lack of diversity jurisdiction. Make use of the cases cited in the Background Principles of Law section above.

business exceed $100,000. In addition, Plaintiff suffered out-of-pocket costs of over $15,000 in computer technician's time in repairing and restoring the system, and replacing the defective Lan2Net software with new intranet networking software. All of these damages occurred at the offices of Plaintiff in St. Louis, Missouri.

11. Defendant failed to deliver a product that met the general and specific requirements of the contract of sale — namely a Y2K compliant intranet networking product, and, therefore, Defendant breached its contract of sale with Defendant.

12. Plaintiff seeks damages for Defendant's breach of contract in an amount to be proved at trial but not less than $115,000, and such further and other relief as the Court deems proper in the circumstances.

WHEREFORE, Plaintiff demands an amount not less than $115,000 from Defendant, and such further and other relief as the Court deems proper in the circumstances.

JURY TRIAL DEMANDED.

RANT, RAVE & BIGSTRETCH, LLP

By:________________________________

J. Clearly Asaro, EDMO # 90210
Lucy O. McKinnis, EDMO # 02112
Newman Piggly Wiggly, EDMO # 86753
1114 Market Street, Suite 2800
St. Louis, Missouri 63101
Phone: 314-555-SU4U
Fax: 314-555-PAYU

Attorneys for Plaintiff St. Mary's Entrepreneur Liquidation Loan Service

BACKGROUND PRINCIPLES OF LAW

(Note: This is not a legal brief or memorandum in support of a motion. It is not in the proper form of an argument section. Do not view it as a sample or model of good argument)

In order to subject a defendant to a judgment in personam, defendant must: (1) have certain minimum contacts with the forum state; and (2) the maintenance of the suit must not offend traditional notions of fair play and substantial justice." Int'l Shoe Co. v. Washington, 326 U.S. 310, 312 (1945).

In order to achieve personal jurisdiction over an out-of-state defendant, Plaintiff must prove: (a) that the defendant committed an act in the state covered by the local Long Arm Statute, Mo. Rev. Stat. 506.500(1), and that the suit arises from this act; and (b) that defendant has a nexus of contacts with Missouri, such that the exercise of personal jurisdiction does not offend Due Process.

A party has minimum contacts with the forum state when the defendant has performed some act by which it has purposefully availed itself of the privilege of conducting activities within the forum state thus invoking the benefits and protections of its laws. Scullin Steel v. National Ry. Utilization Corp., 676 F.2d 309, 314 (8th Cir. 1982), citing Hanson v. Denckla, 357 U.S. 235, 253 (1958). Merely entering into a contract with a forum resident does not provide the requisite contacts between a nonresident defendant and the forum state. Aaron Fere & Sons Co. v. Am. Compressed Steel Co., 564 F.2d 1206, 1211 (8th Cir. 1977).

Here, Mo. Rev. Stat. 506.500(1)(1) pertains to making a contract in Missouri, and § 506.500(1)(2) pertains to doing business in Missouri. Under the Due Process analysis, there is one case from the Eighth Circuit, Marriott v. Cyberworld, 999 F.3d 2345, 2348 (8th Cir. 2000), that states that the maintenance of a web cite can provide a contact with a state that satisfies Due Process if the web site is more than a passive advertisement; in other words, there must be some means for users in the state to interact with the web site, communicate with the company through the site, or place orders through the web site.

---

1. Using the above fact pattern and complaint, draft an Introduction section for **defendant's** motion to dismiss on the basis of lack of diversity jurisdiction.

2. Using the above fact pattern and complaint, draft a Statement of Facts section for **defendant's** motion to dismiss on the basis of lack of diversity jurisdiction.

Chapter 23
MOTIONS FOR SUMMARY JUDGMENT

WRITING EXERCISE

Consider the following set of facts:

MEMORANDUM

TO: [Your Name]

FROM: Rock Cranium

DATE: February 14, 2000

RE: Jiang v. Piao-Liang

SUBJECT: Motion for Summary Judgment

This morning, Judge Kimball denied Pia-Liang's motion to dismiss. We have stipulated to a set of facts with the other side. We must now move for summary judgment.

Please review the stipulation of facts and use it to prepare the memorandum in support of our summary judgment motion. Of course, you can review and make use of the complaint, too.

You should look into the following statute, Utah Code Ann. § 26-31-2 (copied below), that might be important to this case:

Utah Code Ann. § 26-31-2. Sale of Body Parts.

(a) It shall be unlawful, except as provided in subsection (b) of this Code section, for any person, firm, or corporation to buy or sell, to offer to buy or sell, or to assist another in buying or selling or offering to buy or sell a human body or any part of a human body or buy or sell a human fetus or any part thereof.

(b) The prohibition contained in subsection (a) of this Code section shall not apply to:

(1) The purchase or sale of whole blood, blood plasma, blood products, blood derivatives, other self-replicating body fluids or regenerative tissue, or hair, or any action described in Code section 26-31-1;

(2) A gift or donation of a human body or any part of a human body or any procedure connected therewith as provided in Chapter 28 of Title 26 of this Code or to the payment of a processing fee in connection with such gift or donation if such fee is paid to a physician, hospital, bank or storage facility pursuant to Code section 26-28-10(2).

(3) The reimbursement of actual expenses, including medical costs, lost income, and travel expenses, incurred by a living person in giving or donating a part of the person's body;

(4) The payment of financial assistance under a plan of insurance or other health care coverage;

(5) The purchase or sale of human tissue, organs, or other parts of the human body for health sciences education; or

(6) The payment of reasonable costs associated with the removal, storage, or transportation of a human body or any part of a human body given or donated for medical or scientific purposes.

(c) Any person, firm, or corporation convicted of violating subsection (a) of this Code section shall be guilty of a felony and, upon conviction thereof, shall be punished by a fine not exceeding $5,000.00 or by imprisonment for not less than one year nor more than five years, or both.

(Enacted into law, January 30, 1999; effective date, July 1, 1999).

[Note to students: This statute does not exist in Utah. You will not find it in the Utah Code. You will not find any legislative history for this statute in Utah.]

We expect that our opponents will also file a cross-motion for summary judgment using the stipulation that we have worked out. You should be aware of that when you are drafting the memorandum in support of our motion for summary judgment.

R.C.

UNITED STATES DISTRICT COURT
DISTRICT OF UTAH
CENTRAL DIVISION

JIANG CHUANG-PING, Plaintiff, v. PATRICIA PIAO-LIANG DAVIS, A/K/A "PIAO-LIANG", Defendant.	)))))))))	No. 2:99-CV-2345-K (Judge Kimball) JURY TRIAL DEMANDED

COMPLAINT

NOW COMES Plaintiff Jiang Chuang-ping ("Plaintiff"), and for his complaint against Defendant Patricia Piao-Liang Davis, also known as the supermodel "Piao-Liang ("Defendant"), states as follows:

PARTIES

1. Plaintiff is a citizen and resident of the City of San Francisco, State of California, and the United States of America. He is domiciled in the State of California.

2. Defendant Piao-Liang is a citizen and resident of the State of Utah, United States of America, and is domiciled in Provo, Utah, in this District.

JURISDICTION AND VENUE

3. This Court has subject matter jurisdiction over this action under 28 U.S.C. § 1332(a)(1) in that Plaintiff and Defendant have diverse citizenship, and the matter involves over $75,000 in controversy.

4. Personal jurisdiction exists over Defendant because Defendant is a citizen and resident of the State of Utah and of this District and Division and is subject to service of process in this State and District.

5. Defendant and Plaintiff entered into the Contract attached hereto as Exhibit 1 ("Contract") on November 2 and November 4, 1999, respectively.

6. The contract provides for suit to be brought in a federal court in Utah and the Contract is to be governed by Utah law. Contract, section 5.

7. Venue is proper in this district pursuant to the forum selection clause in section 5

of the Contract and pursuant to 28 U.S.C. § 1391(a)(1),(2), in that Defendant is resident and domiciled in this District and Division, and the subject matter of the Contract is present in this District.

COUNT I - BREACH OF CONTRACT

8. On November 2, 1999, Defendant entered into the Contract, promising to deliver to Plaintiff's OB-GYN physician one or more healthy and viable ova from her ovaries at the first available opportunity and no later than June 1, 2000. Upon receipt and successful fertilization and implantation of the egg(s) in Plaintiff's wife's uterus, Plaintiff was to pay Plaintiff by wire transfer the sum of one million United States dollars.

9. On December 18, 1999, Defendant phoned Plaintiff and repudiated the contract by stating that she would not perform her obligations. She then, on that same day, sent by facsimile transmission and U.S. Mail the letter attached hereto as Exhibit 2, again repudiating the Contract and refusing to perform her obligations under the Contract.

10. Plaintiff was and remains ready to perform his obligations under the Contract, and there are no other conditions precedent to the agreement that would prevent its performance.

11. Defendant breached its agreement with Plaintiff by anticipatory repudiation.

12. Plaintiff has no available alternative remedy at law that could replace or compensate Plaintiff for the unique value of the subject matter of the Contract, and seeks specific performance of the Contract, and such further and other relief as the Court deems proper in the circumstances.

COUNT II - SPECIFIC PERFORMANCE

13. Plaintiff realleges the allegations of paragraphs 1-12 of this complaint as though set forth fully in this paragraph.

14. Plaintiff comes to this court seeking equity, with clean hands, and with the equities in his favor. Plaintiff has no available alternative remedy at law. The public policy of this jurisdiction favors the upholding and enforcement of contracts for the provision of a unique subject matter.

15. Defendant has repudiated and breached her obligations under the Contract. The equities and public policy are against Defendant.

16. Plaintiff seeks specific performance of the Contract.

WHEREFORE, Plaintiff requests the Court to order Defendant to deliver to Plaintiff's OB-GYN physician one or more healthy and viable ova from her ovaries at the first available opportunity and no later than June 1, 2000, and to award Plaintiff such further and other relief as the Court deems proper in the circumstances.

JURY TRIAL DEMANDED.

FINLEY, KRUMBLE & BREAKUP, LLP

By:___[signed by Miriam O. McGuinnis]__________
Miriam O. McGuinnis, Ut Bar No. 02112
Thor X. Wang, Ut Bar No. 04523
Xavier Rocque de Hassad, Ut Bar No. 16753
114 Market Street, Suite 2800
Salt Lake City, Utah 84101
Phone: 801-555-SU4U
Fax: 801-555-PAYU

Attorneys for Plaintiff Jiang Chuang-ping

UNITED STATES DISTRICT COURT
DISTRICT OF UTAH
CENTRAL DIVISION

JIANG CHUANG-PING,	)	
	)	
Plaintiff,	)	
v.	)	No. 2:99-CV-2345-K
	)	
PATRICIA PIAO-LIANG DAVIS,	)	
	)	
Defendant.	)	

STIPULATION OF FACTS

The parties to this action, Plaintiff Jiang "Jerry" Chuang-ping ("Jiang") and Defendant Patricia "Piao-Liang" Davis ("Piao-Liang") (collectively, the "parties"), have jointly stipulated to the following facts in this matter:

1. Plaintiff Jiang, age 50, is a naturalized American citizen who owns a controlling interest in and supervises four factories producing computer memory chips in Taibei, Republic of China. Jiang was born in Taibei in 1950. He immigrated to the United States in 1979, and was naturalized as a U.S. citizen in 1984.

2. Jiang is the nephew of the late General and President of the R.O.C., Jiang Ji-shi, better known to the world as Chiang Kai-shek.

3. Defendant Patricia Piao-Liang Davis, age 20, is an international fashion model who goes by the professional name "Piao-Liang."

4. Piao-Liang was born in Nanjing, P.R.C. in 1979, but was orphaned at four months of age, and was adopted at six months of age by Clifford and June Davis, U.S. citizens, and raised in Provo, Utah. Piao-Liang is a naturalized citizen of the United States, and lives in Provo, Utah.

5. From January 10, 1999, to December 19, 1999, Piao-Liang was listed as one of several "super-models" who offered their unfertilized ova for auction on an Internet site known as Dezyner-Genes.com. Piao-Liang received several offers to purchase her eggs, but she never accepted any of these offers.

6. On October 28, 1999, Piao-Liang was approached at West Lake in Hangzhou by Jiang. Jiang explained to Piao-Liang that his wife was infertile, and he was interested in purchasing an ovum from Piao-Liang. Jiang offered Piao-Liang $1 million for an egg. Piao-Liang and Jiang orally agreed to the transaction on October 28, 1999.

7. After further negotiation and discussion of terms between the parties and their attorneys, Piao-Liang and Jiang entered into a written contract on November 2 and November 4, 1999, respectively. A true and correct copy of this contract is attached hereto as Exhibit 1 (the "Contract").

8. The Contract provides for Piao-Liang to deliver to Plaintiff's OB-GYN physician one or more healthy and viable ova from her ovaries at the first available opportunity and no later than June 1, 2000.

9. Upon receipt and successful fertilization and implantation of the egg(s) in Jiang's wife's uterus, Jiang was to pay Piao-Liang by wire transfer the sum of one million United States dollars.

10. The process for obtaining the ova from Piao-Liang is an invasive surgical procedure. The ripe ova are removed from her ovaries through laparoscopy or by ultrasound-guided needle aspiration through her abdomen or vagina.

11. No personal contact or interaction between Jiang and Piao-Liang is required in order for Piao-Liang to perform the Contract.

12. On December 18, 1999, Piao-Liang telephoned Jiang and sent a letter by facsimile transmission and U.S. Mail to Jiang to inform him that the Contract must be terminated and that performance cannot occur. A true and correct copy of the letter sent by Piao-Liang to Jiang is attached to the Complaint as Exhibit 2.

Respectfully submitted,

FINLEY, KRUMBLE & BREAKUP, LLP
By:_[signed by Miriam O. McGuinnis]___
Attorneys for Plaintiff Jiang Chuang-ping

DOTT, TEE & CROSSEYE P.C.
By:_[signed by Sandra Glib Gabber]______
Attorneys for Defendant Patricia Piao-Liang Davis

Purchase and Sale Contract

WHEREFORE, Mr. Jerry Jiang Chuang-Ping (Buyer) and Ms. Patricia Piao-Liang Davis (Seller) wish to enter into an agreement for the transfer of at least one egg from Seller's ovaries to Buyer for the purpose of fertilization of the egg and implantation in Buyer's wife; and

WHEREFORE, the parties, Buyer and Seller, in consideration of the mutual promises stated herein and for other good and valuable consideration; and

WHEREFORE, the parties, Buyer and Seller, wish to complete this transaction at the earliest practicable time, and in no event later than June 1, 2000;

Then the parties covenant and agree to the following:

1. At the earliest practicable opportunity, and in no event later than June 1, 2000, in New York City, NY or Salt Lake City, UT, or at any other mutually agreeable location, Seller shall deliver to Buyer's OB-GYN physician one or more healthy and viable ova (i.e., eggs) from her ovaries.

2. Upon receipt and successful fertilization of the egg(s), the egg(s) are to be implanted in Buyer's wife's uterus,

3. After successful implantation of the fertilized egg(s) in Buyer's wife's uterus, without miscarriage, for twenty-one days, Buyer shall pay Seller by wire transfer to Osmond National Bank, Account No. 100223456 owned by Seller, the sum of one million United States dollars.

4. In the event that conditions 2 and 3 cannot be successfully completed with the initial supply of the egg(s) from Seller, Seller shall, within six weeks of notification by facsimile or U.S. mail by Buyer of the failure of conditions 2 or 3, supply one or more additional healthy and viable eggs to Buyer's OB-GYN physician in New York City, NY or Salt Lake City, UT, and shall continue to supply eggs in the manner described in this paragraph every six weeks until successful completion of conditions 2 and 3 of this contract.

5. Should any dispute between the parties arise under this agreement, the parties, Buyer and Seller, agree that all disputes shall be resolved in litigation that shall be filed in a state or federal court in the State of Utah and all conditions and terms and obligations of this contract shall be governed by and interpreted under Utah law.

Signed by Buyer:

_____[signed by Jiang]_______
Jerry Jiang Chuang-ping
Date: November 4, 1999
Taibei, R.O.C.

Signed by Seller:

___[signed by Piao-Liang]______
Patricia Piao-Liang Davis
Date: November 2, 1999
New York, NY

Exhibit 1

Assuming that there is not other state or federal law that might affect this action, no cases are on point, and that the Utah Sale of Body Parts Act (quoted above) is potentially applicable:

1. Using the above fact pattern, statute, complaint, and stipulation, draft an Introduction section for **defendant's** motion for summary judgment that will argue that the Utah Sale of Body Parts Statutes makes the contract illegal and void.

2. Using the above fact pattern, statute, complaint, and stipulation, draft a Statement of Facts section for **defendant's** motion for summary judgment that will argue that the Utah Sale of Body Parts Statutes makes the contract illegal and void.

3. Draft 3-5 paragraphs of the Argument section of **defendant's** motion for summary judgment, arguing that the Utah Sale of Body Parts Statutes makes the contract illegal and void.

4. Assume that you represent the plaintiff. Using the above fact pattern, statute, complaint, and stipulation, draft an Introduction section for **plaintiff's** opposition to defendant's motion for summary judgment, that argues that the Utah Sale of Body Parts Statutes does not apply to this transaction and does not make the contract illegal and void.

5. Draft a Statement of Facts section for **plaintiff's** opposition to defendant's motion for summary judgment, that argues that the Utah Sale of Body Parts Statutes does not apply to this transaction and does not make the contract illegal and void.

6. Draft 3-5 paragraphs of the Argument section of **plaintiff's** opposition to defendant's motion for summary judgment, arguing that the Utah Sale of Body Parts Statutes does not apply to this transaction and does not make the contract illegal and void.

Chapter 25
APPELLATE BRIEFS

WRITING EXERCISES

1. Correct these questions presented for review to comply with public policy drafting style favored by courts of last resort:

   a. Whether plaintiff/petitioner Jones is entitled to display a flag upside down hanging outside his dorm window at defendant/respondent State University of New York at Albany in full view of passers by and nearby street traffic?

   b. Whether petitioner Smith is entitled to use the image and likeness of respondent Governor Arnold Black on a campaign poster critical of Black's prior career as an actor and body-builder that is designed to draw up support for an opposition gubernatorial candidate running against Black in the latest recall election in California?

   c. Whether petitioner Jones is entitled to bring a strict products liability failure to warn claim against respondent Medtechies, Inc., the manufacturer of a mechanical heart valve that is operating normally and performing all of its intended functions but which is one of a production line of heart valves that have a 90% failure rate, which fact caused severe emotional distress to Jones when she learned of this fact after undergoing implantation of the device?

2. Rephrase the statements below twice—once to create a summary of argument for petitioner's brief and the second time to create a summary of argument for respondent's brief. Feel free to elaborate on the facts and law by creating details missing from the account, but do not change the basic facts stated below:

   a. Plaintiff/respondent Humpty Dumpty sat on a wall. Humpty Dumpty had a great fall. All of defendant/petitioner King's horses and all of his men could not put Humpty Dumpty back together again. However, Humpty Dumpty signed a waiver before scaling the wall that spelled out: King shall not be liable for any fall off the wall except for a fall caused by the intentional misconduct or gross negligence of King or King's agents and employees. The trial court directed a verdict in King's favor, and Humpty Dumpty appealed.

b. Nathan Detroit allegedly runs the oldest, established, permanent floating crap game in New York. On one evening, a visiting dignitary from Joliet, Illinois, going by the name "Big Jule," interrupted the game by introducing dice that didn't have any spots on them. After a brief confrontation, Big Jule produced a handgun and menaced all of the patrons of the crap game with it. Most of them left the game. Nathan has sued Big Jule for assault and intentional interference with business relations. Big Jule's summary judgment motion and motion for directed verdict were denied, and the action proceeded to a jury verdict in favor of Nathan. Big Jule appealed.

c. Clark Adams wrote a novel entitled "Revenge" and used it to lure publisher Kinsey Milhaughn down to his private island estate in South Carolina, where he pretended to be a paraplegic in order to gain Kinsey's sympathies. He bedded Kinsey and let her husband, Ryan Foster, know so as to force Ryan to come down to the island, where Clark caught Ryan in an elaborate trap in a well inside an abandoned sawmill, where Clark left Ryan to die. Clark explained to Ryan that he was punishing him for stealing the plot of Clark's first novel when the two of them were roommates in Key West, Florida, after both of them graduated from the creative writing program of the University of Tennessee. Ryan was rescued from the well by a passing sheriff's deputy. Kinsey left Ryan and moved in with Clark. Ryan has sued Clark for alienation of affection, fraud, and gross negligence. Ryan's action was dismissed for failure to state a claim, and he appealed.

3. Rephrase these thesis headings to make them meaningful and helpful to the reader. Do not forget the "because" part:

a. Scout is entitled to judgment as a matter of law on her dog bite claim.

b. Personal jurisdiction exists over Duane in Idaho.

c. The Bank received the money transfer under circumstances that render retention just and appropriate.

d. The DMCA is a content neutral regulation of Centron's website.

4. Rephrase these sections from a controlling authority to create the argument section of an appellate brief. Do this twice—once for petitioner's brief and the second time for respondent's brief. Feel free to elaborate on the authorities cited but do not change the

true meaning and effect of the legal standards stated below.

a. A parody creating a likelihood of confusion may be subject to a trademark infringement action. *Cliffs Notes*, 886 F.2d at 494 (confusing parodies are "vulnerable under trademark law"); *L.L. Bean, Inc. v. Drake Publishers, Inc.*, 811 F.2d 26, 32 n. 3 (1st Cir.) (confusing parodies "implicate[ ] the legitimate commercial and consumer protection objectives of trademark law"), *cert. denied and appeal dismissed*, 483 U.S. 1013, 107 S.Ct. 3254, 97 L.Ed.2d 753 (1987). There is no simple, mechanical rule by which courts can determine when a potentially confusing parody falls within the First Amendment's protective reach. Thus, "in deciding the reach of the Lanham Act in any case where an expressive work is alleged to infringe a trademark, it is appropriate to weigh the public interest in free expression against the public interest in avoiding consumer confusion." *Cliffs Notes*, 886 F.2d at 494. "This approach takes into account the ultimate test in trademark law, namely, the likelihood of confusion as to the source of the goods in question." *Id.* at 495 (internal quotations omitted).

In applying this balancing test, we begin with the recognition that parody serves as a "humorous form of social commentary and literary criticism that dates back as far as Greek antiquity." *Bean*, 811 F.2d at 28. Balducci purports to comment on several matters, including environmental pollution and Anheuser-Busch's brand proliferation. The First Amendment's protection of social commentary generally, and parody in particular, is certainly implicated in this case. "The fact that parody can claim legitimacy for some appropriation does not, of course, tell either parodist or judge much about where to draw the line." *Campbell v. Acuff-Rose Music, Inc.*, 510 U.S. 569, ----, 114 S.Ct. 1164, 1172, 127 L.Ed.2d 500 (1994). "The benefit to the one making the parody ... arises from the humorous association, not from public confusion as to the source of the marks." *Jordache Enters.*, 828 F.2d at 1486.

Anheuser-Busch, Inc. v. Balducci Publications, 28 F.3d 769, 776 (8th Cir. 1994)

b. Texas follows the ordinary principles of common law for money had and received claims:

> The question, in an action for money had and received, is to which party does the money, in equity, justice, and law, belong. All plaintiff need show is that defendant holds money which in equity and good conscience belongs to him. Again, it has been declared that a cause of action for money had and received is less restricted and fettered by technical rules and formalities than any other form of action. It aims at the abstract justice of the case, and looks solely at the inquiry, whether the defendant holds money, which belongs to the plaintiff.

> *Staats v. Miller*, 150 Tex. 581, 243 S.W.2d 686, 687-88 (1951) (quoting 58 C.J.S., Money Received § 4a, and *United States v. Jefferson Elec. Mfg. Co.*, 291 U.S. 386, 402-03, 54 S.Ct. 443, 78 L.Ed. 859 (1934) (internal quotations omitted)).
>
> Most recently, an intermediate Texas court explained that "[t]o maintain an action for money had and received, [a plaintiff must] establish that the [defendant] held money which in equity and good conscience belonged to [the plaintiff].... Money had and received is an equitable doctrine applied to prevent unjust enrichment." *Miller-Rogaska, Inc. v. Bank One, Texas, N.A.*, 931 S.W.2d 655, 662 (Tex.App. Dallas 1996).

Bank of Saipan v. CNG Financial Corp., 380 F.3d 836, 840 (5th Cir. 2004)

c. The duty at issue here is the obligation of the dog owner to control his pet in a way that protects the health and safety of others. We conclude that Montana law imposes such a duty under Mont. Code Ann. § 27-1- 715(1) (1981), which provides:

> The owner of any dog which shall without provocation bite any person while such person is on or in a public place or lawfully on or in a private place, including the property of the owner of such dog, located within an incorporated city or town shall be liable for such damages as may be suffered by the person bitten regardless of the former viciousness of such dog or the owner's knowledge of such viciousness.

Under this statute a private citizen comparably situated to Airman Harris could have a duty to control his pet. Montana law specifies that a duty exists only if there is a foreseeable risk of injury. *Schafer v. State Department of Institutions*, 592 P.2d 493, 495 (Mont. 1979). An injury such as Catherine suffered was reasonably foreseeable. Harris therefore had a state law duty enforceable under the FTCA.

The standard of reasonable care in performing that duty is specified in Base Regulation 125-5, which requires the owner to maintain total control of the animal at all times, either by confining it or through voice control. It is obvious on the undisputed facts that Harris failed to satisfy this standard. For whatever reason, Harris's dog was neither confined nor under voice control when it attacked Catherine.

Lutz v. United States, 685 F.2d 1178, 1184 (9th Cir. 1982)

Part II
Writing Assignments

I. SINGLE CASE ANALYSIS ASSIGNMENT

INSTRUCTIONS TO STUDENTS

- Prepare a report of your analysis of the facts and issues presented in the assignment memo on the next page. You are to analyze the facts described in the assignment memo and any issues raised by these facts in light of the case Nelson v. Lewis that you read in Appendix A. Do not do any additional research. Do not look up any of the cases or other materials cited in Nelson v. Lewis. When you cite the case, cite it as Nelson v. Lewis, p. XXX (i.e., whatever page number you are citing to).

- **Page limit: two (2) pages, double spaced**. Follow the style and formatting requirements presented in the syllabus. Write or type your name in the upper right corner of the first page. Do not draft an entire office memorandum (something we will discuss later in Chapter 7), just draft the following parts: Start your paper with your Thesis for the analysis in a heading, such as:

A. Lillohman will be able to recover on a claim against Deowner for his injuries because . . . [give your reasons].

or

A. Lillohman will not be able to recover on a claim against Deowner for his injuries because . . . [give your reasons].

Then write a Rule section (1-2 paragraphs) laying out the rule(s) you learned in the Nelson case, and an Explanation section that explains how the Nelson court interpreted and applied the rule(s). Then write an Application section (1 paragraph) in which you apply the Nelson case to the new facts described in the assignment memo. Finish off the paper with a one sentence Thesis Restated as Conclusion. You need not worry about the concept of explanatory synthesis discussed in Chapter 6 because you only have one case (Nelson v. Lewis) to apply to the new facts. Do not draft any other sections (such as Issue, Facts, etc.).

MEMORANDUM

TO: Iben A. Partner

FROM: M. Mary Quitecontrary

DATE: August 30, 2004

RE: Iben Lillohman/Litigation Matters (C1234/56789)

SUBJECT: Potential claim arising from dog encounter

Our firm needs to analyze the claim of an existing client. I know you and your students are familiar with the prevailing authority on this issue in Illinois, Nelson v. Lewis. Please have your students predict Lillohman's chances of success in a claim against Chaim Deowner based on the following facts:

Dr. Iben Lillohman ("Lillohman") is an 80 year old gentleman who lives on the top floor of an apartment building in Belleville, Illinois. He is very near sighted and uses a cane to help navigate around. Recently, some new neighbors, Chaim Deowner and his family, moved onto Lillohman's floor. The Deowners have a large Presa Canario (Canary Islands) dog named Bobo. Lillohman was never formally introduced to the Deowners or to Bobo, but shortly after the Deowners moved in, Lillohman encountered Bobo as the dog was laying down quietly by the elevator in the hallway while Chaim Deowner was carrying some groceries into his apartment down the hall. Lillohman, who couldn't see very well, walked up to Bobo laying quietly on the carpet and looked down at the dog, but what Lillohman thought he was seeing was a large bulge in the carpet in front of the elevator. Not wanting to trip on the "bulge," Lillohman prodded it rather firmly with his cane. Bobo, after being prodded in the side by Lillohman's cane, jumped to his feet, knocking the cane out of Lillohman's hand, and reared up placing his heavy front paws on Lillohman's chest, and barked in Lillohman's face several times. Lillohman was so startled that he had a heart attack and fell down on his back with the dog on top of him, injuring his hip and elbow. Fortunately, Chaim Deowner called 911 and paramedics were able to rush Lillohman to a hospital where he recovered from his injuries. Later, Chaim Deowner told a neighbor, Esau Nothing, that he thought Bobo had jumped on Lillohman and barked at him because the dog thought Lillohman wanted to play, and that is what Bobo does with Deowner's children when they are playing.

Please evaluate Lillohman's chances of success in light of Nelson v. Lewis should Lillohman decide to sue Chaim Deowner for his injuries.

II. CLOSED MEMO - EXAMPLE 1

INSTRUCTIONS TO STUDENTS

- Draft an office memorandum as described in Chapter 7. Report your analysis of the facts and the issue presented in the assignment memo below in light of the following statute and cases:

  17 U.S.C. § 107

  Campbell v. Acuff-Rose Music, Inc., 510 U.S. 569 (1994)

  Dr. Seuss Enterprises, L.P. v. Penguin Books USA, Inc., 109 F.3d 1394 (9th Cir. 1997)

  Leibovitz v. Paramount Pictures Corp., 137 F.3d 109 (2d Cir. 1998)

  Rogers v. Koons, 960 F.2d 301 (2nd Cir. 1992)

  Steinberg v. Columbia Pictures Industries, Inc., 663 F. Supp. 706 (S.D.N.Y. 1987)

  Do not do any additional research. Do not look up any of the cases and materials cited within the cases listed above. **Page limit: 5-7 pages.**

- Follow the style and formatting requirements for an office memorandum presented in the syllabus and in the course text. Write or type your name in the upper right corner of the first page. Cite cases by the first named party and a page reference, as in: Campbell at 581; Rogers at 310.

MEMORANDUM

TO: Iben A. Partner

FROM: Carol Ng Book

DATE: September 18, 2004

RE: Friends of Alternative Marriage/National Midnight Star v. FOAM (C1234/00001)

SUBJECT: Use of Parody Defense in Copyright Infringement Case

Our firm needs to analyze the claim of a new client, Friends of Alternative Marriage ("FOAM"). Please have your students predict FOAM's chances of success in raising a defense of "parody" to allegations of copyright infringement.

In 2003, FOAM started fund raising efforts to support reformation of state laws regarding gay marriage and civil unions. One of the materials developed in this effort was a poster attached here as Exhibit 1. On the poster, FOAM used two copyrighted imaged owned by the expose magazine National Midnight Star ("NMS"). The images relate to famed rock star Britney Swords' 55 hour marriage to Jason Alexoleander that started and finished in Las Vegas. One image was Britney Swords' marriage license, which FOAM altered by adding an image of Swords floating in the background of the license, and added the text, "Valid for 55 hours or less" in red block letters at the bottom of the license. The other image was an alleged photograph of Swords and Alexoleander and an unidentified couple at Sword's and Alexoleander's wedding. FOAM altered this image by adding text of "Little White Wedding Chapel, Las Vegas" over the heads of the persons in the photographs. FOAM surrounded the two borrowed images with quotations from anti-gay marriage advocates in bold typeface, and added its own message: "By all means, stop gay marriage. Don't let it make marriage less sacred" in large, red, block lettering as follows:

"Marriage is a sacred institution between a man and a woman. Today's decision of the Massachusetts Supreme Judicial Court violates this important principle."
— President George W. Bush

"We must amend the Constitution if we are to stop a tyrannical judiciary from redefining marriage to the point of extinction."
— Focus on Family

"The time is now. If you don't do something about this, then you cannot in 20 years—when you see the American public disintegrating and you see our enemies overtaking us because we have no moral will—you remember that you did nothing."
— Sandy Rios, President of the Concerned Women for America

". . . [I]t is absolutely unthinkable that Christians should allow marriage to become the province of the secular state. To do so would be a profanation, a sin of irreverence to the sacrament and disobedience to the Lord's Church."
- Father Mateo

BY ALL MEANS - STOP GAY MARRIAGE
DON'T LET IT MAKE MARRIAGE LESS SACRED

FOAM did not ask NMS for permission to use the images. NMS sued FOAM in the United States District Court for the Southern District of New York for copyright infringement.

We first need to evaluate whether FOAM can claim that these works are a bona fide parody as that term is interpreted and defined under 17 U.S.C. § 107 on "fair use" of copyrighted works. There are several elements to fair use, but I want your students to focus on the first element: whether the nature and purpose of FOAM's work is a parody. Your students should assume that FOAM's poster does infringe on the copyrights of NMS unless FOAM can prove that it made a "fair use" of the images through parody.

Your students should not focus on the second half of element 1 – FOAM's motives were for commercial gain (they were using the images for fund raising, although FOAM itself is a public interest, not for profit organization). Nor should they research and write about elements 2-4. Element 2 on the nature of the copyrighted work appears to be a non-issue here (the images here are publicly known, expressive works and are copyrightable). Element 3 is undisputed – FOAM took the two images in their entirety. Element 4 should be ignored until we do more fact finding on the effect on the market for the original work. All of the above issues are going to be moot if FOAM is found to have failed the parody definition under the "nature and purpose of the use" element under 17 U.S.C. § 107.

Your students should answer the legal question: Is the nature and purpose of FOAM's use a parody within the meaning of 17 U.S.C. § 107?

- CNB

CLOSED MEMO ASSIGNMENT
REQUIREMENTS FOR THE OUTLINE

Your outline should contain:

1. The Issue

2. A preliminary Thesis that answers the question (one sentence, rather than a full Conclusion/Brief Answer)

3. The Main Rule section with citations to the authorities that provide the rules that govern the Issue and any explanatory and interpretive rules on the main Rules (do not worry about the form of the cites, just use the name of plaintiff from the case and a page reference; e.g., Steinberg at 709)

4. If you intend to write any sub-TREATs, please provide the sub-Theses for the sub-TREATs

Your outline should not contain a Conclusion/Brief Answer, Statement of Facts, Explanation sections or Application sections. Thus, explanatory synthesis will not appear in the outline.

There is a 2 page limit for the outline. Most outlines will fit on one page.

CLOSED MEMO - EXAMPLE 2

INSTRUCTIONS TO STUDENTS

- Draft an office memorandum as described in Chapter 7. Report your analysis of the facts and the issue presented in the assignment memo below in light of the following cases:

  Hume, 157 N.J. Super 310

  Hill, 342 N.J. Super 273

  Taylor, 152 N.J. 490

  Buckley, 111 N.J. 355

  Lascurain, 349, N.J. Super 251

  Griffin, 337 N.J. Super 15

  Hart, 308 N.J. Super 487

  Do not do any additional research. Do not look up any of the cases and materials cited within the cases listed above. **Page limit: 5-7 pages.**

- Follow the style and formatting requirements for an office memorandum presented in the syllabus and in the course text. Write or type your name in the upper right corner of the first page. Cite cases by the first named party and a page reference, as in: Hart at 488; Griffin at 19.

MEMORANDUM

TO: File

FROM: Joseph Partner

RE: Elle Forrest's Intentional Infliction of Emotional Distress Claim

---

Today I got a phone call from Elle Forrest. Elle is a first year law student at Pinnacle Law School in Newark, NJ. She is only two weeks into the semester and is considering either immediately transferring, or perhaps even dropping out of law school altogether – all due to the behavior of her contracts professor, Professor Socrates. Before she does that, however, her father – he and I were law school roommates – encouraged her to call me to see whether she might file a lawsuit in New Jersey against her professor.

The facts that Elle reported to me are as follows. On the very first day of class, Professor Socrates called on Elle (she didn't have her hand raised) and asked her several questions about a case she read the night before. Right off the bat, he used a derogatory tone and stood ominously close to her as he asked the first question. To her answer, he said, "What kind of moronic answer is that? You are wasting my time and your classmates' time and this school's time if you think you are going to be a good lawyer!"

Understandably shocked, Elle tried to restate her answer, but Professor Socrates cut her off by waving his hand just inches from her face and exclaiming, "Can someone else please help me out, here? Ms. Forrest is obviously useless to us."

On the second day of Contracts, Elle was terrified. She switched her seat to the middle of a row (she'd been on the end the first day and thought she'd be less conspicuous in the middle).

Professor Socrates called on several other students that day and, although he was certainly curt and rude, he did not, in Elle's opinion, hurl the kind of insults at her classmates that he had at her the first day. Near the end of the class, however, he apparently noticed Elle again and called on her again by stating in a sarcastic manner, "Class, let's see what illuminating thoughts Ms. Forrest might have amidst all that air in her head today."

Elle tried to laugh the comment off, but she felt tears welling up in her eyes. She attempted to answer but stopped mid-stream, her voice noticeably cracking. Professor Socrates pressed on, stating "Do you expect us to believe you are serious about being a lawyer? No one will ever take you seriously with that Jersey girl look of yours and the accent to boot! So when did you decide to give up being a Springsteen groupie and take a stab at a real career?" Elle had no idea how he knew she was indeed from New Jersey, and she did not take the criticisms of her home state lightly.

On the third day of class, there was a picture of Elle hanging on the outside front door of the classroom. It was her picture from the Pinnacle face book – but it had been blown up and a tall cone hat was drawn onto it with the word "DUNCE" printed across it. Underneath was the caption: "Typical Jersey Girl." The picture had her name under it and could be seen not only by everyone in her section, but anyone passing by that area of the hall. She suspected that Socrates had posted it – or at the very least someone that had heard his comments.

Elle did not go to class that day, but instead went to the Dean's office and complained about Professor Socrates. The Dean told her that Professor Socrates was one of the school's finest professors – in fact, they had managed to lure him away from NYU the year before. At NYU, he had the reputation of being "really hard on the students" and, at times, acerbic. There had been some complaints from students – especially female students – that he was particularly vicious towards them, but no formal disciplinary action had ever been taken against him. The Dean told Elle that Pinnacle did not permit students to switch sections.

Right now, all she wants to do is drop out, having been convinced that law school is not for her. Her father wants her at least to consider switching schools and, as I noted above, to consider fighting back.

As a result of her encounters with Professor Socrates, Elle has suffered great mental anguish. She has been unable to sleep well or eat well, and she is unable to do any of the work that she needs to do for any of her classes. She is already two weeks behind and is panicking. She cries uncontrollably every morning.

She reported her angst to a psychiatrist – albeit a doctor she has been seeing for two years for separate matters. The therapist prescribed sleeping pills to help her cope with the new stress, and she told me (at Elle's request) that she would be willing to sign an affidavit stating that Elle has been experiencing increased anxiety and increased depression since starting law school.

I have never had a case like this before but seem to recall reading in the *NJ Law Journal* that New Jersey recognizes the tort of intentional infliction of emotional distress. I suspect that Elle may be able to bring such a claim against Professor Socrates, but before I discuss that with her, I need more information. If Elle were to bring this claim, what is the likelihood that we could survive what I imagine would be an immediate claim by the professor for dismissal?

III. OPEN MEMO - EXAMPLE 1

INSTRUCTIONS TO STUDENTS

- Research and draft an office memorandum as described in Chapter 7. Report your analysis of the facts and the issues presented in the assignment memo and the additional information that is developed from your meeting with the client. **Page limit: 8 pages.**

- Follow the style and formatting requirements for an office memorandum presented in the syllabus and in the course text. Write or type your name in the upper right corner of the first page. Our client, Victor Chandelbise, is not willing to pay for computerized research. Accordingly, you must do all legal research using the library and may not use Lexis, Westlaw, or any other computer-assisted legal research service on this assignment. However, once you have read an authority in a reporter or other print source, you may use Lexis or Westlaw to print that authority, rather than using a photocopy machine. In addition, once you have read an authority in its print form, you may use Shepard's (Lexis) or KeyCite (Westlaw) to print out a list of authorities citing your original authority. Except as expressly provided in this paragraph, you may not use Lexis, Westlaw, or any other computer-assisted legal research service for other any purpose, including reading cases you have not first read in their print form, conducting searches, or "clicking through" to authorities cited in Shepard's, KeyCite, or any other on-line source. Please note that both Westlaw and Lexis provide the ability to track your accounts to determine if you have violated the guidelines laid out in this paragraph.

MEMORANDUM

TO: Iben A. Partner

FROM: Carol Ng Book

DATE: October 16, 2003

RE: Victor Chandelbise/Products Claim (C68901/89012)

SUBJECT: Possible suit arising from death of wife

I am turning to you once again because your students did such a good job on that FOAM matter, and their work was so nice and concise—only five pages! Once again, our firm needs to analyze the claim of a new client, Victor Emmanuel Chandelbise. Please have your students determine whether Victor can bring an action against Homenides de Histangua Hospital and the surgeon and inventor, Dr. Finache. I've arranged for Victor to visit your law school the week of October 20 so that your students can interview him to gather information on the case. Attached is an article from the newspaper that gives some details about the event:

ST. LOUIS POST-DISPATCH

St. Louis woman dies from heart valve failure

Date: September 15, 2003
By: Romain Tournel

At 3:30 a.m. on September 14, a St. Louis woman, Yvonne Chandelbise, died from cardiac arrest en route to Barnes Hospital. The cause of the 43 year old woman's death was apparently related to her Keltic VII heart valve. Chandelbise was one of the first recipients of the Keltic VII heart valve, invented by famed local surgeon Dr. Walter Finache and a team of scientists working at the Homenides de Histangua Hospital in Webster Groves, Missouri.

Chandelbise received the heart valve in March 2003 after several years of severe cardiovascular problems. Her husband, Victor Emmanual Chandelbise, reported that the valve worked fine for several months, but then his wife started hearing audible clicking as the valve opened and shut. Soon after, on September 12, Yvonne saw a news story on Spinline news program that reported that several Keltic VII heart valves had failed, causing fragments of the lining of the valves to break off and to spin into the bloodstream causing fatalities. The story mentioned that the failure of the valves often was preceded by audible sounds from the valves.

Yvonne was greatly disturbed by the news, and suffered several panic attacks on September 12 and 13 following the airing of the news story. On the night of September 13, Yvonne awoke in the middle of the night and her husband reported that she "was in a full blown panic attack," and she made statements to the effect that the clicking sounds from her heart valve were getting louder. She then went into cardiac arrest, and died en route to the hospital.

This was the first such report of a potential failure-related death attributable to the Keltic VII heart valve in the state of Missouri. Neither Dr. Finache nor Homenides de Histangua Hospital chose to comment on this matter. Yvonne Chandelbise is survived by her husband and a son, Camille Chandelbise.

OPEN MEMO ASSIGNMENT

REQUIREMENTS FOR THE OUTLINE

Your outline should contain:

1. The Issues

2. Preliminary Theses that answer the issues (one sentence, rather than a full Conclusion/Brief Answer)

3. The Main Rule sections with citations to the authorities (in correct, Bluebook citation form) that provide the rules that govern each issue and any explanatory and interpretive rules on the main rules.

4. Any sub-Theses identifying sub-TREATs that you intend to write

5. Any sub-Rules that go in the sub-TREAT sections that you intend to write, with citations to the authorities that provide the rules that govern the sub-issues and any explanatory and interpretive rules on the sub-Rules

Your outline should not contain a Conclusion/Brief Answer, Statement of Facts, Explanation sections or Application sections. Thus, explanatory synthesis will not appear in the outline.

There is no page limit, but I don't think anyone will need more than **3 pages** double spaced for this.

OPEN MEMO - EXAMPLE 2

INSTRUCTIONS TO STUDENTS

- Research and draft an office memorandum as described in Chapter 7. Report your analysis of the facts and the issues presented in the assignment memo and the additional information that is developed from your meeting with the client. **Page limit: 8 pages.**

- Follow the style and formatting requirements for an office memorandum presented in the syllabus and in the course text. Write or type your name in the upper right corner of the first page.

OFFICE OF THE UNITED STATES ATTORNEY
DISTRICT OF ARIZONA

INTRA-OFFICE MEMORANDUM

TO: Intern

FROM: Dakota Parker
Assistant United States Attorney, Criminal Division

DATE: September 30, 2004

RE: Tala Granger
Possible Endangered Species Act Violation

Officers from the Arizona Game and Fish Department recently arrested Ms. Tala Granger for shooting a Mexican gray wolf while she was camping near Sedona in the Coconino National Forest.

Based on our analysis of the factual evidence thus far and on a forensic investigation by the Game and Fish Department, we have determined that:

[1] The gray wolf in question is an endangered species in Arizona;

[2] The wolf in question was <u>not</u> part of an "experimental population;" and

[3] The bullet shot from Ms. Granger's gun was in fact the cause of the wolf's death.

However, we are still not sure that criminal prosecution is warranted under the Endangered Species Act.

Accordingly, we would like you to prepare a memorandum addressing each of the following two issues:

Whether, assuming that the wolf in question is endangered and not part of an "experimental population," Ms. Granger committed a criminal violation of the Endangered Species Act by killing it; and

Whether Ms. Granger has a valid claim for self-defense or defense of her dog based on her description of the events that transpired.

Your memorandum should be limited to the two issues identified above and should predict the outcome of any criminal prosecution.

IV. PERSUASIVE VS. OBJECTIVE WRITING ASSIGNMENT

INSTRUCTIONS TO STUDENTS

1. Choose one of the following topics:

    Your favorite/ least favorite movie or TV show or play
    Your favorite/ least favorite entertainer or sports figure
    Your favorite/ least favorite sport or sporting event
    Your favorite/ least favorite politician
    Your favorite/ least favorite pet or animal
    Your favorite/ least favorite work of art or style (school, genre, etc.) of art
    Pete Rose's potential admission to the Baseball Hall of Fame
    Media coverage of celebrity trials (Michael Jackson, Martha Stewart, etc.)

2. Write an objective, fair, and balanced description of the topic in no more than 1-2 paragraphs, double-spaced. What are the merits and demerits?

3. Then write a persuasive account (again in no more than 1-2 paragraphs, double-spaced) trying to convince the reader that your take on the topic is correct and the reader should adopt it; *e.g.*, persuading the reader that X is the least/most desirable Y around. Advocate and argue for your position and only your position.

    Total pages not to exceed 1.5 pages double-spaced. Turn in hard copy only.

V. MOTION TO CHANGE VENUE

INSTRUCTIONS TO STUDENTS

- Research and draft a memorandum in support of motion to change venue or a memorandum in opposition to motion to change venue depending on whichever side you sign up to represent. **Page limit: 7 pages.**

- Follow the style and formatting requirements presented in the syllabus and in the course text. ***Do not follow the local rules for California state courts.*** You do not need to prepare a signature block and certificate of service, but if you elect to do them, they will not count against your page limit (i.e., you may put them on page 8, but nothing else can go on page 8). Write or type your name in the upper right corner of the first page. Perform any research you think necessary to prepare the work, **including** any **computerized, on-line, or Internet** legal research tools and databases.

MEMORANDUM

TO: Junior Associate

FROM: Senior Partner

DATE: January 19, 2004

RE: Newsflash Creative Media v. Arnold Black

SUBJECT: Motion to Change Venue

Defendant Arnold Black is a famous film star and the governor of California. Since becoming a major film star some fifteen years ago, he has received an enormous amount of attention from national and international media outlets. In the last three years, he has been on the cover of over 380 newspapers and more than 250 news magazines. He has received close to $90 million from his acting and product promotions in 2003 alone.

Plaintiff Newsflash Creative Media is a corporation formed by two artists, Jeffrey Toons and Peter Tax, who both live in the Castro district of San Francisco, California. The day after Black, appearing on the Tonight Show with Jay Sterno, announced his bid to become governor of California in the recall election of October 2003, Newsflash Creative Media produced and started selling a line of T-shirts depicting Black in various poses from his days as an actor or bodybuilder. Each T-shirt sells for $15. There are four versions of the T-shirts, each depicting Arnold Black with the phrase "Newsflash" at the top, and a message, presumably about Black, at the bottom, including: "Robot, Statesman, Governor," "Governor Arnold," "Governor Terminator," and "Der Groppenfuhrer." Arnold Black did not authorize the use of his image on T-shirts and no one associated with Black gave Newsflash the rights either. [NOTE: The potential claims of the owners of the copyrights of these images are not at issue in this assignment].

Arnold Black saw one of the T-shirts at a fundraising event and became furious. He immediately had his lawyers draft up a threatening cease and desist letter to Newsflash Creative Media. The letter demanded that Newsflash cease the distribution or sale of any T-shirts, and any other article that features the likeness of Arnold Black produced without the consent of Black. The letter also ordered Newsflash to retrieve and destroy all existing examples of such items, within 10 days, or Black would sue Newsflash under California law for violation of Mr. Black's right of publicity.

Newsflash Creative Media, being no stranger to controversy, got the jump on Mr. Black and sued him in the Superior Court of California, County of San Francisco for declaratory judgment under the California Right of Publicity statute.

Our first task is draft a court brief (Memorandum in Support/Opposition) regarding the Motion to Change Venue filed by Defendant Black. See attached court file. Use the declarations in the court file when you are drafting your memorandum.

SP

[NOTE: You should consider all documents below to be properly signed. All documents in this packet are part of the record in this case and may be cited and discussed by either side, plaintiff or defendant.]

IN THE SUPERIOR COURT OF CALIFORNIA
IN AND FOR THE COUNTY OF SAN FRANCISCO

JEFFREY TOONS AND PETER TAX, d/b/a NEWSFLASH CREATIVE MEDIA, Plaintiff, v. ARNOLD BLACK, Defendant.	)))))))))	 No. 03-C-9345 Judge Lillian K. Sing JURY TRIAL DEMANDED

COMPLAINT

NOW COME Plaintiffs Jeffrey Toons and Peter Tax, together doing business as Newsflash Creative Media ("Plaintiffs"), and for their complaint against Defendant Arnold Black ("Defendant"), state as follows:

PARTIES

1. Plaintiffs Jeffrey Toons and Peter Tax are citizens and domiciliaries of the City of San Francisco, San Francisco County, State of California. Plaintiffs Jeffrey Toons and Peter Tax operate a graphic design business known as Newsflash Creative Media. All of their operations, facilities and equipment are located in San Francisco, California. 90% of their sales occur in San Francisco.

2. Defendant Arnold Black is a citizen of the State of California, and is domiciled in the City of Sacramento, Sacramento County, California.

VENUE

3. Venue is proper in this district pursuant Cal. Civ. Proc. Code § 395(a) because the threatened injuries to Plaintiffs' constitutional rights and a substantial part of the alleged injuries to Defendant's persona and publicity rights occurred in the County of San Francisco.

COUNT I—DECLARATORY JUDGMENT

4. On August 6, 2003, Defendant announced on the Tonight Show with Jay Sterno that he would be a candidate for governor of California in the recall election scheduled for

October 2003.

5. The next day, August 7, 2003, Plaintiffs introduced and began selling a line of T-Shirts depicting Black in various poses from his days as an actor or bodybuilder. Each T-shirt sells for $15. There are four versions of the T-shirts, each depicting Arnold Black with the phrase "Newsflash" at the top, and a message about Black at the bottom, including: "Robot, Statesman, Governor," "Governor Arnold," Governor Terminator," and "Der Groppenfuhrer" (the "T-Shirts").

6. The T-Shirts report newsworthy information on a matter of great public interest and thus are protected from claims under the California Right of Publicity Act.

7. In addition, the T-Shirts are parodies and as such they are protected from claims under the California Right of Publicity Act.

8. Defendant has no claim against Plaintiffs under the California Right of Publicity Act based on the creation and sale of the T-Shirts.

9. On December 1, 2003, Defendant sent by facsimile transmission and U.S. Mail a letter threatening Plaintiffs and demanding that Plaintiffs cease and desist production, distribution and sale of the T-Shirts, and any other "derivative works" containing the image of Defendant without the consent of Defendant. The letter also calls for Plaintiffs to destroy the T-Shirts and other "derivative works" now and in the future possession of Plaintiffs. The letter threatened a lawsuit within ten days of the letter if its terms were not followed.

10. An actual case and controversy exists between Plaintiffs and Defendant based on the letter and the threats of legal action concerning Plaintiffs' T-Shirts contained therein. Plaintiffs will suffer irreparable harm to its rights under the California and United States Constitutions' free expression clauses.

WHEREFORE, Plaintiffs request the Court to order a declaratory judgment in favor of Plaintiffs and against Defendant, ordering and decreeing that Plaintiffs have the right to produce, sell, and distribute the T-Shirts and to award Plaintiffs such further and other relief as the Court deems proper in the circumstances.

JURY TRIAL DEMANDED.

SERRANO, MAPPLETHORPE, & RODIN, P.C.

By:____

Andres Serrano Cal. Bar No. 6157980
Robert Mapplethorpe Cal. Bar No. 6215678
Auguste Rodin Cal. Bar No. 6223344
111 Embarcadero Place
San Francisco, California, 90603-6110
Phone: 800-555-ARTY
Fax: 800-555-SU4U

Attorneys for Plaintiff Newsflash Creative Media

Filed: December 8, 2003

IN THE SUPERIOR COURT OF CALIFORNIA
IN AND FOR THE COUNTY OF SAN FRANCISCO

JEFFREY TOONS AND PETER TAX, d/b/a NEWSFLASH CREATIVE MEDIA, Plaintiff,	)	No. 03-C-9345 Judge Lillian K. Sing
v.	)	
ARNOLD BLACK, Defendant.	)	

MOTION TO CHANGE VENUE

NOW COMES defendant Arnold Black ("Defendant"), and moves this Court pursuant to Cal. Civ. Proc. Code § 396a and Cal. Rules of Court, Rule 326, for a change of venue to transfer this action to the Superior Court of California, County of Los Angeles. In support of this motion, Defendant states:

Defendant recognizes that venue is appropriate in this county because a portion of the injuries to Defendant and the imagined injuries to Plaintiffs did occur or are threatened to occur in this County. Nevertheless, as described in the attached Declarations of Arnold Black and Scott Skiptracer, this action should be transferred for the convenience of the parties and witnesses and the ends of justice. Venue is appropriate in the Superior Court of California, County of Los Angeles because defendant resides and works there and all of his witnesses, documents, and the greatest and most important on-going injuries from Plaintiffs' actions are occurring there.

WHEREFORE, Defendant Arnold Black prays the Court will transfer this action to the Superior Court of California, County of Los Angeles, and award Defendant costs and expenses and such further and other relief as the Court deems appropriate in this matter.

Respectfully Submitted,

ASHCROFT, ROBERTSON, & HATCH
By:________________________________

Orrin Hatch Cal. Bar No. 5322445
601 South Figueroa Street, Suite 200
Los Angeles, CA 90068
Phone: (888) 555-9900 Fax: (888) 555-9901

Attorneys for Defendant Arnold Black

IN THE SUPERIOR COURT OF CALIFORNIA
IN AND FOR THE COUNTY OF SAN FRANCISCO

JEFFREY TOONS AND PETER TAX, d/b/a NEWSFLASH CREATIVE MEDIA, Plaintiff, v. ARNOLD BLACK, Defendant.	)))))))))	 No. 03-C-9345 Judge Lillian K. Sing

DECLARATION OF ARNOLD BLACK

I, Arnold "Arnold" Black, of lawful age, do swear under penalty of perjury of the laws of the United States and the State of California that I have first hand information concerning the following and the following information is true and correct:

1. I am 56 years old. I am a citizen and resident of California. I reside at 18 Sargent Shriver Road, Brentwood, CA 90006.

2. My acting career and my own personal business and promotional activities are based in Los Angeles, California. Although I currently am the Governor of California, I have not moved to Sacramento because there is no governor's mansion there, and so when I am forced to be in Sacramento on state business, I conduct my activities from temporary offices and residence in a presidential suite of the Hyatt Regency Hotel that sits across the street from the Capitol Building in Sacramento. I have not changed my domicile to Sacramento County. I conduct a great deal of the business of governor from my residence in Los Angeles County.

3. All of the witnesses to my personal affairs, promotions and publicity — including my agent, Guy Bombastic, my personal manager, Bea Flexible, and my accountant and financial planner, Bill Checker — are residents of Los Angeles. None of these witnesses are amenable to process in the County of San Francisco. All of the documents, exhibits, and other evidence of my fame, advertising, and promotional activities are located in Los Angeles. The film industry and media from which I derive the greatest part of my income and fame are based in Los Angeles County.

4. As governor and a famous actor, I travel a great deal, and on occasion I have traveled to San Francisco County. However, my current, grave responsibilities as the governor of this state in the middle of the worst budget crisis in state history will make it very difficult and

inconvenient to repeatedly travel to San Francisco for the purposes of this lawsuit. If this suit were transferred to the Superior Court of California, County of Los Angeles, I and my witnesses could fully participate in this suit without interrupting my manifestly important duties as the chief executive of this great state.

FURTHER DECLARANT SAYETH NAUGHT.

Sworn to under penalty of perjury on this 29th day of December 2003.

____

Arnold Black

IN THE SUPERIOR COURT OF CALIFORNIA
IN AND FOR THE COUNTY OF SAN FRANCISCO

JEFFREY TOONS AND PETER TAX, d/b/a NEWSFLASH CREATIVE MEDIA,	)	
Plaintiff,	)	No. 03-C-9345
v.	)	Judge Lillian K. Sing
ARNOLD BLACK,	)	
Defendant.	)	

DECLARATION OF SCOTT SKIPTRACER

I, Scott Skiptracer, of lawful age, do swear under penalty of perjury of the laws of the United States and the State of California that I have first hand information concerning the following and the following information is true and correct:

1. I am 38 years old. I am a citizen and resident of San Francisco, California.

2. I am a duly licensed and authorized private investigator and process server in the State of California. I am licensed and authorized to do business in the County of San Francisco, County of Oakland, County of Sacramento, and County of Marin, California.

3. I was engaged by Defendant Black to gather information regarding the above captioned matter.

4. Plaintiffs Jeffrey Toons and Peter Tax (currently doing business under the name Newsflash Creative Media) are citizens of California and residents of San Francisco. They rent space, which appears to be a studio and work space, in the Castro District of San Francisco at 234 Castro Alley, San Francisco, CA 90609. The T-Shirts bearing the image of Defendant Black ("T-Shirts") are produced at this site.

5. In a three week surveillance of the Plaintiffs in December 2003 and January 2004, I observed that some of their sales are conducted at the Castro District studio, but the vast majority of sales are conducted by "runners" and "mules" employed by the Plaintiffs who carry the T-Shirts to various tourist spots and sports events in and around San Francisco, Oakland, and San Jose.

6. The Plaintiffs also are selling the T-Shirts in Los Angeles County. On four occasions (the Rose Bowl Game, and three Lakers games), I observed agents of the Plaintiffs

selling the T-Shirts outside these sporting events. Sales were made, and on each occasion the entire stock of T-Shirts carried by Plaintiffs' agents sold out in less than a hour.

7. Both plaintiffs, Jeffrey Toons and Peter Tax, are well-known artists in California and across the nation and world. Both Toons and Tax are active participants in the Los Angeles County art world and art business.

8. Jeffrey Toons broke into fame in 1988 with his Solo Exhibition at the Sonnabend Gallery in New York City. He has been called, "The most influential artist of his generation" by Art Review in April 2003. He has had several shows at the Daniel Weinberg Gallery, Los Angeles and Los Angeles Contemporary Museum of Art and Los Angeles County Museum of Art. In one day in January 2004, I saw Toons' work and reproductions of his work for sale in four different art galleries in Los Angeles County, including the internationally renowned David DeSanctis Contemporary Art gallery on Melrose Place and Jeannette Peek's Silent Poetry gallery on Rodeo Drive.

9. Peter Tax has been famous since the 1960's for his "Cosmic '60s" style, with its distinctive line work and bold color combinations. Tax's Cosmic '60s art, with its transcendental imagery, captured the imagination of the entire generation and catapulted the young artist to fame and fortune. Tax was suddenly on numerous magazine covers, including Life Magazine, and appeared on national TV. Tax's visual impact on the 1960s has often been compared to the influence the Beatles had with their music. He has been Official Artist for five Super Bowls and the World Cup USA, including events that took place in Los Angeles, California. In one day in January 2004, I saw Tax's work for sale in 14 different art galleries and poster shops in Los Angeles County, including the David DeSanctis Contemporary Art gallery on Melrose Place and Jeannette Peek's Silent Poetry gallery on Rodeo Drive.

10. According to the Judicial Council of California, 2003 Court Statistics Report, available at http://www.courtinfo.ca.gov/reference/3_stats.htm, there is no significant difference in civil case time from filing to disposition between the Superior Court of Los Angeles County and the Superior Court of San Francisco County.

FURTHER DECLARANT SAYETH NAUGHT.

Sworn to under penalty of perjury on this 12th day of January 2004.

____

Scott Skiptracer

VI. MOTION TO DISMISS FOR LACK OF PERSONAL JURISDICTION

INSTRUCTIONS TO STUDENTS

- Research and draft a memorandum in support of motion to dismiss or a memorandum in opposition to motion to dismiss depending on whichever side you sign up to represent. **Page limit: 7-8 pages.**

- Follow the style and formatting requirements presented in the syllabus and in the course text. ***Do not follow the local rules for the United States District Court for the Western District of Tennessee.*** You do not need to prepare a signature block and certificate of service, but if you elect to do them, they will not count against your page limit (i.e., you may put them on page 8, but nothing else can go on page 8). Write or type your name in the upper right corner of the first page of one of your final copies. Perform any research you think necessary to prepare the work, **including** any **computerized, on-line, or Internet** legal research tools and databases.

MEMORANDUM

TO: Junior Associate

FROM: Senior Partner

DATE: January 24, 2005

RE: Newsflash Creative Media v. Arnold Black

SUBJECT: Motion to Dismiss

Defendant Arnold Black is a famous film star and the governor of California. Since becoming a major film star some fifteen years ago, he has received an enormous amount of attention from the United States and world press. In the last three years, he has been on the cover of over 380 newspapers and more than 250 news magazines. He has received close to $90 million from his acting and product promotions in 2004 alone.

In October 2003, he left the field of entertainment and joined the field of politics when he was elected governor in a special recall election in which then governor Kray Davis was recalled and Black was elected. Since then, Black, a Republican, has become a very popular speaker and fund-raiser at Republican events, and was one of the featured speakers at the Republican National Convention in New York City in August 2004 leading up to the 2004 national election.

Tennessee was not a swing state in the 2004 national election, but it did have a close senatorial race between the incumbent Lamar Alexoleander, a Republican, and Democrat Kristin Flore, the daughter of former Vice-President Al Flore. In October 2004, Governor Black made two appearances in Tennessee, one in Memphis and one in Nashville, to appear at rallies and fund raisers for Republican candidates including the Republican senatorial candidate, Alexoleander. At the fund raising events, Black succeeded in raising $2 million for Republican candidates including Alexoleander.

Plaintiff Newsflash Creative Media is a corporation owned and controlled by two artists, Jeffrey Toons and Peter Tax, who both live in Memphis, Tennessee. On October 3, 2004, the day after Black appeared on the Tonight Show with Jay Sterno and announced that he was going on a sweep of the south, including his stops in Tennessee, Newsflash Creative Media produced and started selling a line of T-shirts depicting Black in various poses from his days as an actor or bodybuilder. Each T-shirt sells for $20, of which $10 was to cover most of the cost of the T-shirts and the other $10 was donated to the Tennessee Democratic Party.

There were four versions of the T-shirts, each depicting Arnold Black with the phrase "Newsflash" at the top, and a message, presumably about Black, at the bottom, including: "Robot,

Statesman, Governor," "Governor Arnold," Governor Terminator," and "Der Groppenfuhrer." On the back of each T-shirt was the following message:

Republicans?
Get real, Tennessee!
Vote Democrat

Newsflash Creative Media
(800) 818-8200
newsflash1@newsflash.net

Each word of the message was in the same large, bold typeface.

Arnold Black did not authorize the use of his image on T-shirts and no one associated with Black gave Newsflash the rights either. [NOTE: The potential claims of the owners of the copyrights of these images are not at issue in this assignment].

Arnold Black saw one of the T-shirts at the fund raising event in Nashville and became furious. He immediately had his lawyers draft up a threatening cease and desist letter to Newsflash Creative Media. The letter demanded that Newsflash cease the distribution or sale of any T-shirts, or any other article that features the likeness of Arnold Black produced without the consent of Black, and retrieve and destroy all existing examples of such items, within 11 days, or Black would sue Newsflash for violation of Black's right of publicity.

Newsflash Creative Media, being no stranger to controversy, got the jump on Black and sued him in the United States District Court for the Western District of Tennessee for declaratory judgment under the Tennessee Personal Rights Protection Act.

Our first task is to draft a court brief (Memorandum in Support/Opposition) regarding the Motion to Dismiss for Lack of Personal Jurisdiction filed by Defendant Black. See attached court file. NOTE that the only issue to brief in the motion is whether Arnold Black had sufficient minimum contacts with the State of Tennessee such that it would or would not violate the Due Process Clause of the United States Constitution to sue Black in Tennessee. Use the declarations in the court file when you are drafting your memorandum. Tennessee law and federal law (under the Due Process Clause) applies to this motion.

[NOTE: You should consider all documents below to be properly signed. All documents in this packet are part of the record in this case and may be cited and discussed by either side, plaintiff or defendant. Plaintiff granted Defendant an appropriate extension of time to file his motion to dismiss and memorandum in support so do not make any issue of the timeliness of the filing.]

UNITED STATES DISTRICT COURT
WESTERN DISTRICT OF TENNESSEE
WESTERN DIVISION

NEWSFLASH CREATIVE MEDIA,	)	
	)	
Plaintiff,	)	No. 04-C-9345 (BAD)
v.	)	
	)	
ARNOLD BLACK,	)	JURY TRIAL DEMANDED
	)	
Defendant.	)	

COMPLAINT

NOW COMES Plaintiff Newsflash Creative Media ("Newsflash"), and for its complaint against Defendant Arnold Black ("Defendant"), state as follows:

PARTIES

1. Plaintiff Newsflash is a corporation organized and existing under the laws of the State of Tennessee and has its place of incorporation and headquarters and principal place of business in the State of Tennessee. Its shareholders and officers, Jeffrey Toons and Peter Tax, both are citizens and domiciliaries of the City of Memphis, State of Tennessee. Newsflash is a graphic design business. All of its operations, facilities, and equipment are located in Memphis, Tennessee.

2. Defendant Arnold Black is a citizen of the State of California, and is domiciled in the City of Sacramento, Sacramento County, California.

VENUE AND JURISDICTION

3. Venue is proper in this district pursuant to 28 U.S.C. § 1391 because the threatened injuries to Newsflash's constitutional rights and a substantial part of the alleged injuries to Defendant's persona and publicity rights occurred in the City of Memphis in the State of Tennessee and within the territory of the United States District Court for the Western District of Tennessee.

4. Jurisdiction is appropriate in this Court under 28 U.S.C. § 1332 because the citizenship of the plaintiff and the defendant is diverse, and over $75,000 is in controversy in the suit.

COUNT I—DECLARATORY JUDGMENT

5. On October 2, 2004, Defendant announced on the Tonight Show with Jay Sterno that he would visit Memphis and Nashville, Tennessee in order to support Republican Party candidates for United States Senator and other offices in the national election scheduled for November 2004. The next day, October 3, 2004, Newsflash introduced and began selling a line of T-Shirts depicting Black in various poses from his days as an actor or bodybuilder. There are four versions of the T-shirts, each depicting Arnold Black with the phrase "Newsflash" at the top, and a message about Black at the bottom, including: "Robot, Statesman, Governor," "Governor Arnold," Governor Terminator," and "Der Groppenfuhrer" (the "T-Shirts"). Newsflash sold and distributed these shirts in Memphis and Nashville, Tennessee in order to raise money for the Democratic Party in Tennessee and as a form of political commentary on the propriety of an violent action film star supporting Republican candidates for public office in Tennessee. Defendant Black succeeded in raising over $2 million for the Republican Party in his sojourn in Tennessee, while Newsflash raised $80,000 for the Tennessee Democratic Party with sales of 8,000 T-shirts.

6. The T-Shirts report newsworthy information on a matter of great public interest and thus are protected from claims under the Tennessee Personal Rights Protection Act of 1984. Although the 2004 National Election is over, Newsflash continues to sell the T-shirts and desires in the future to continue to sell the T-shirts to raise money for the Tennessee Democratic Party and to continue commenting on the Republican Party's activities in Tennessee and its out-of-state supporters, including Defendant Black.

7. Defendant has no claim against Newsflash under the Tennessee Personal Rights Protection Act of 1984 based on the creation and sale of the T-Shirts.

8. On October 15, 2004, Defendant sent by facsimile transmission and U.S. Mail a letter threatening Newsflash and demanding that Newsflash cease and desist production, distribution, and sale of the T-Shirts and any other works containing the image of Defendant without the consent of Defendant. The letter also calls for Newsflash to destroy the T-Shirts and other "derivative works" now and in the future possession of Newsflash. The letter threatened a lawsuit within eleven days of the letter if its terms were not followed.

9. An actual case and controversy exists between Newsflash and Defendant based on the letter and the threats of legal action concerning Newsflash's T-Shirts contained therein. Newsflash will suffer irreparable harm to its rights under the Tennessee and United States Constitutions' free expression clauses if Defendant carries out his threats.

WHEREFORE, Newsflash requests the Court to order a declaratory judgment in favor of Newsflash and against Defendant, ordering and decreeing that Newsflash has the right to produce, sell, and distribute the T-Shirts and to award Newsflash such further and other relief as the Court deems proper in the circumstances.

JURY TRIAL DEMANDED.

SERRANO, MAPPLETHORPE, & RODIN, P.C.

By:____

Andres Serrano TN Bar No. 6157980
Robert Mapplethorpe TN Bar No. 6215678
Auguste Rodin TN Bar No. 6223344
139A Beale Street
Memphis, Tennessee 38103
Phone: 800-555-ARTY
Fax: 800-555-SU4U

Attorneys for Plaintiff Newsflash Creative Media

Filed: October 17, 2004

UNITED STATES DISTRICT COURT
WESTERN DISTRICT OF TENNESSEE
WESTERN DIVISION

NEWSFLASH CREATIVE MEDIA,	)	
	)	
Plaintiff,	)	No. 04-C-9345 (BAD)
v.	)	Hon. Bernice A. Donald
	)	
ARNOLD BLACK,	)	
	)	
Defendant.	)	

MOTION TO DISMISS

NOW COMES defendant Arnold Black ("Defendant"), and moves this Court pursuant to Fed. R. Civ. P. 12(b)(2) to dismiss this action for lack of personal jurisdiction over the Defendant In support of this motion, Defendant states:

Defendant has never conducted business in Tennessee and has only visited Tennessee twice in his life. These two occasions had nothing to do with any business or other activity of the Defendant that would create a nexus with the State of Tennessee such that the Court may exercise personal jurisdiction over Defendant in this state and judicial district consistent with the minimum contacts requirement of the Due Process Clause of the United States Constitution.

WHEREFORE, Defendant Arnold Black prays the Court will dismiss this action and award Defendant costs and expenses and such further and other relief as the Court deems appropriate in this matter.

Respectfully Submitted,

ASHCROFT, ROBERTSON, & HATCH

By:______________________________

Orrin Hatch TN Bar No. 5322445
201 North Main Street, Suite 200
Memphis, TN 38103
Phone: (888) 555-9900
Fax: (888) 555-9901

Attorneys for Defendant Arnold Black

UNITED STATES DISTRICT COURT
WESTERN DISTRICT OF TENNESSEE
WESTERN DIVISION

NEWSFLASH CREATIVE MEDIA,	)	
	)	
Plaintiff,	)	No. 04-C-9345 (BAD)
v.	)	Hon. Bernice A. Donald
	)	
ARNOLD BLACK,	)	
	)	
Defendant.	)	

DECLARATION OF ARNOLD BLACK

I, Arnold "Arnold" Black, of lawful age, do swear under penalty of perjury of the laws of the United States and the States of California and Tennessee that I have first hand information concerning the following and the following information is true and correct:

1. I am 57 years old. I am a citizen and resident of California. I reside at 18 Sargent Shriver Road, Brentwood, CA 90006.

2. My acting career and my own personal business and promotional activities are based in Los Angeles, California. Although I currently am the Governor of California, I have not moved to Sacramento because there is no governor's mansion there, and so when I am forced to be in Sacramento on state business, I conduct my activities from temporary offices and residence in a presidential suite of the Hyatt Regency Hotel that sits across the street from the Capitol Building in Sacramento. I have not changed my domicile to Sacramento County. I conduct a great deal of the business of governor from my domicile and residence in Los Angeles County, California.

3. I only have visited Tennessee twice in my life. The first visit took place in 1980 when I posed with Ms. Dolly Bustamonte for a country music calendar designed to raise money for St. Jude's Research Hospital. The latest visit took place on October 3 and 4, 2004, when I agreed to appear at political events for friends who were candidates for public office in Tennessee. I visited Memphis on October 3 and Nashville on October 4, and then I left the State. I have not returned.

4. I have no other personal or professional contacts in Tennessee. Although I was reimbursed approximately $1,200 for my travel and hotel expenses for my appearance with Dolly Bustamonte twenty five years ago in 1980, I received no benefit from my most recent visit to Tennessee. I transacted no business while in Tennessee in 2004. I received no compensation for my visit in 2004.

5. This lawsuit between Newsflash and me has nothing whatsoever to do with my first visit to Tennessee in 1980, and is only tangentially related to my visit in October 2004. In fact, this action is related to the unauthorized exploitation of my valuable persona from my film career which is based in California. The relevant facts show that the actual and threatened injuries to my persona and publicity rights occurred in California, and therefore this action arises in and has a nexus with me as defendant in the State of California but not the State of Tennessee.

FURTHER DECLARANT SAYETH NAUGHT.

Sworn to under penalty of perjury on this 12th day of December 2004.

____

Arnold Black

UNITED STATES DISTRICT COURT
WESTERN DISTRICT OF TENNESSEE
WESTERN DIVISION

NEWSFLASH CREATIVE MEDIA, Plaintiff,	)	No. 04-C-9345 (BAD)
v.	)	Hon. Bernice A. Donald
ARNOLD BLACK, Defendant.	)	

DECLARATION OF PETER TAX

I, Peter Tax, of lawful age, do swear under penalty of perjury of the laws of the United States and the State of Tennessee that I have first hand information concerning the following and the following information is true and correct:

1. I am 67 years old. I am a citizen and resident of Memphis, Tennessee.

2. Tennessee was not a swing state in the 2004 national election, but it did have a close senatorial race between the incumbent Lamar Alexoleander, a Republican, and Democrat Kristin Flore, the daughter of former Vice-President Al Flore.

3. On October 3 and 4, 2004, Governor Arnold Black made two appearances in Tennessee, one in Memphis and one in Nashville, to appear at rallies and fund raisers for Republican candidates including the Republican senatorial candidate, Alexoleander. At the fund raising events, Black succeeded in raising $2 million for Republican candidates including Alexoleander.

4. Plaintiff Newsflash Creative Media ("Newsflash") is a corporation owned and controlled by two artists, Jeffrey Toons and me, Peter Tax, who both live in Memphis, Tennessee. We are the sole shareholders and officers of Newsflash.

5. On October 3, the day after Black appeared on the Tonight Show with Jay Sterno and announced that he was going on a sweep of the south, including his stops in Tennessee, Newsflash Creative Media produced and started selling a line of T-shirts ("T-shirts") depicting Black in his more familiar roles as a violent action film star and a chauvinistic bodybuilder. Each T-shirt sells for $20, of which $10 was to cover most of the cost of the T-shirts and the other $10 was donated to the Tennessee Democratic Party.

6. There were four versions of the T-shirts, each depicting Arnold Black with the phrase "Newsflash" at the top and a message about Black at the bottom, including: "Robot, Statesman, Governor," "Governor Arnold," Governor Terminator," and "Der Groppenfuhrer." On the back of each T-shirt was the following political message directly relevant to the political situation in Tennessee then and now:

Republicans?
Get real, Tennessee!
Vote Democrat

Newsflash Creative Media
(800) 818-8200
newsflash1@newsflash.net

7. Newsflash sold and distributed these shirts in Memphis and Nashville, Tennessee in order to raise money for the Democratic Party in Tennessee and as a form of political commentary on the propriety of a violent, chauvinistic, action film star supporting Republican candidates for public office in Tennessee. Newsflash raised $80,000 for the Tennessee Democratic Party with sales of 8,000 T-shirts.

8. The T-Shirts reported and continue to report newsworthy information on a matter of great public interest. Although the 2004 National Election is over, Newsflash continues to sell the T-shirts and desires in the future to continue to sell the T-shirts to raise money for the Tennessee Democratic Party and to continue commenting on the Republican Party's activities in Tennessee and its out-of-state supporters, including Defendant Black.

9. Arnold Black apparently saw one of the T-shirts at a fund raising event in Nashville and became furious. He immediately had his lawyers draft up a threatening cease and desist letter to Newsflash Creative Media. The letter demanded that Newsflash cease the distribution or sale of any T-shirts, or any other article that features the likeness of Arnold Black produced without the consent of Black, and retrieve and destroy all existing examples of such items, within 11 days, or Black would sue Newsflash for violation of Mr. Black's right of publicity.

10. This letter has put Newsflash and me and Mr. Toons in the position of risking costly, destructive litigation or ceasing from exercising our own Constitutional rights to engage in current, relevant political speech. I am chilled by the Defendant's letter and the threats contained therein.

FURTHER DECLARANT SAYETH NAUGHT.

Sworn to under penalty of perjury on this 22th day of December 2004.

____

Peter Tax

VI. APPELLATE BRIEF

INSTRUCTIONS TO STUDENTS

- **Page limit:** **First Draft of Argument section must not exceed twelve (12) pages. Final Draft of Argument section and Conclusion section must not exceed twelve (12) pages, and the entire appellate brief must not exceed twenty-four (24) pages not including the Caption cover page and the back.**

- Newsflash's counsel are to research and draft an Appellant's brief and Black's counsel are to research and draft an Appellee's brief. Follow the style and formatting requirements presented in the syllabus and in the course text (chapter 25). ***Do not follow the local rules for the United States Court of Appeal, Sixth Circuit.*** Your final appellate brief must contain in the order listed below the following sections described in Chapter 25: Caption cover page, Questions Presented for Review (using the "notice" method), Table of Contents, Table of Authorities, Statement of Jurisdiction, Standard of Review, Statement of the Case, Summary of the Argument, Argument, and Conclusion. The Statement of Jurisdiction and Standard of Review sections may appear on the same page. All other sections must begin on a new page. Do not prepare a signature block and certificate of service. If you choose to include a short appendix (1-6 pages), it will not count in the page limit. This assignment packet shall be referred to as the **Record on Appeal**, and citations to the record shall take the form (R.pg.#) as in: (R.8) or (R.3, ¶ 2). The cover and back of appellant's brief should be light blue and the cover and back of appellee's brief should be red. Briefs should be stapled into a booklet with three staples on the left side. That is the only acceptable form of binding. Write or type your name in the upper right corner of the cover of your brief.

MEMORANDUM

TO: Junior Associate

FROM: Senior Partner

DATE: February 17, 2005

RE: Newsflash v. Black

SUBJECT: Appeal

The court denied Defendant Arnold Black's motion to dismiss. Defendant Black and Plaintiff Newsflash worked out a Stipulation of Facts. Defendant asserted a counterclaim against Plaintiff for violation of the Tennessee Personal Rights Protection Act. Plaintiff and Defendant each filed cross-motions for summary judgment asserting their claims, counterclaims, and defenses under the Tennessee Personal Rights Protection Act, Tenn. Code Ann. §§ 47-25-1103, 47-25-1105, and 47-25-1107 and the U.S. Const. amend. I, freedom of expression clause. The motions assumed that Plaintiff's works violated Defendant's right of publicity, and so the motions focused on Plaintiff's affirmative defenses regarding its freedom to use Black's image in a publication of news or parody.

The court granted Defendant's motion and denied Plaintiff's motion (see attached order and judgment). Plaintiff is filing an appeal.

SP

[NOTE TO STUDENTS: You should consider all documents below to be properly signed. All documents in this packet are part of the record in this case and may be cited and discussed by either side, Newsflash or Black. Another word to the wise: Courts rarely use correct Bluebook citation form, so it is never advisable to copy a citation form you see in an order or opinion from a court.]

UNITED STATES DISTRICT COURT
WESTERN DISTRICT OF TENNESSEE
WESTERN DIVISION

NEWSFLASH CREATIVE MEDIA,	)	
	)	
Plaintiff,	)	No. 04-C-9345 (BAD)
v.	)	
	)	
ARNOLD BLACK,	)	
	)	
Defendant.	)	

STIPULATION OF FACTS

The parties in the above captioned matter, Plaintiff Newsflash Creative Media ("Newsflash"), and Defendant Arnold Black ("Black"), hereby stipulate and agree to the following facts:

1. Plaintiff Newsflash is a corporation organized and existing under the laws of the State of Tennessee and has its place of incorporation and headquarters and principal place of business in the State of Tennessee. Its shareholders and officers, Jeffrey Toons and Peter Tax, both are citizens and domiciliaries of the City of Memphis, State of Tennessee. Newsflash is a graphic design business. All of its operations, facilities, and equipment are located in Memphis, Tennessee.

2. Defendant Arnold Black is a citizen of the State of California, and is domiciled in the City of Sacramento, Sacramento County, California.

3. Venue is proper in this district pursuant to 28 U.S.C. § 1391 because the threatened injuries to Newsflash's constitutional rights and a substantial part of the alleged injuries to Black's persona and publicity rights occurred in the City of Memphis in the State of Tennessee and within the territory of the United States District Court for the Western District of Tennessee.

4. Jurisdiction is appropriate in this Court under 28 U.S.C. § 1332 because the citizenship of the Newsflash and the Black is diverse, and over $75,000 is in controversy in the suit.

5. On October 2, 2004, Black announced on the Tonight Show with Jay Sterno that he would visit Memphis and Nashville, Tennessee in order to support Republican Party candidates for United States Senator and other offices in the national election scheduled for November 2004.

6. The next day, October 3, 2004, Newsflash introduced and began selling a line of T-

Shirts (the "T-Shirts") depicting Black in various poses from his days as an actor or bodybuilder. Newsflash sold and distributed these shirts in Memphis and Nashville, Tennessee in order to raise money for the Democratic Party in Tennessee. There were four versions of the T-shirts, each depicting Arnold Black with the phrase "Newsflash" at the top, and a message at the bottom, including: "Robot, Statesman, Governor," "Governor Arnold," "Governor Terminator," and "Der Groppenfuhrer." On the back of each T-shirt was the following message:

Republicans?
Get real, Tennessee!
Vote Democrat

Newsflash Creative Media
(800) 818-8200
newsflash1@newsflash.net

Each word of the message was in the same large, bold typeface.

7. The parties concede and stipulate that Newsflash knowingly used the image and likeness of Defendant Black without Black's consent, and that Newsflash used it on articles of clothing that were sold for purposes of fund raising and for solicitation of donations as described in Tennessee Personal Rights Protection Act, Tenn. Code Ann. § 47-25-1105(a).

8. The parties concede that Black's image is valuable and has distinctive publicity value within the meaning of the Tennessee Personal Rights Protection Act, Tenn. Code Ann. § 47-25-1103.

9. Defendant Black succeeded in raising over $2 million for the Republican Party in his October visit to Tennessee, while Newsflash raised $80,000 for the Tennessee Democratic Party with sales of 8,000 T-shirts. The $80,000 raised is net of the amount retained by Newsflash to cover the price of production of the shirts. Newsflash retained no net profits from the T-shirt sales.

10. Although the 2004 National Election is over, Newsflash continues to sell the T-shirts and desires in the future to continue to sell the T-shirts to raise money for the Tennessee Democratic Party and to continue commenting on the Republican Party's activities in Tennessee and its out-of-state supporters, including Defendant Black.

11. On October 15, 2004, Black sent by facsimile transmission and U.S. Mail a letter demanding that Newsflash cease and desist production, distribution, and sale of the T-Shirts and any other works containing the image of Black without the consent of Black. The letter also calls for Newsflash to destroy the T-Shirts and other "derivative works" now and in the future possession of Newsflash. The letter discussed a lawsuit that would be filed within eleven days of the letter if the letter's terms were not followed.

12. An actual case and controversy exists between Newsflash and Black.

Respectfully submitted,

SERRANO, MAPPLETHORPE, & RODIN, P.C.

By:____

Andres Serrano TN Bar No. 6157980
Robert Mapplethorpe TN Bar No. 6215678
Auguste Rodin TN Bar No. 6223344
139A Beale Street
Memphis, Tennessee 38103
Phone: 800-555-ARTY
Fax: 800-555-SU4U

Attorneys for Plaintiff Newsflash Creative Media

ASHCROFT, ROBERTSON, & HATCH

By:____

Orrin Hatch TN Bar No. 5322445
201 North Main Street, Suite 200
Memphis, TN 38103
Phone: (888) 555-9900
Fax: (888) 555-9901

Attorneys for Defendant Arnold Black

Dated: February 1, 2005

UNITED STATES DISTRICT COURT
WESTERN DISTRICT OF TENNESSEE
WESTERN DIVISION

NEWSFLASH CREATIVE MEDIA,	)	
	)	
Plaintiff,	)	No. 04-C-9345 (BAD)
v.	)	
	)	
ARNOLD BLACK,	)	
	)	
Defendant.	)	

ORDER AND JUDGMENT

The parties each have moved for summary judgment based on a stipulation of facts. The parties' stipulation and each party's motion assumes that the T-shirts created by the Plaintiff unfairly violate Defendant Black's rights of publicity under the Tennessee Personal Rights Protection Act unless Plaintiff's affirmative defenses under Tenn. Code Ann. § 47-25-1107 and U.S. Const. amend. I for freedom of expression (1) to discuss news and current affairs, and (2) to express parody as a form of comment and criticism against Defendant exonerate Plaintiff from liability. Thus, this case presents two issues: (1) Whether Plaintiff is exonerated from liability under Tenn. Code Ann. § 47-25-1107 or U.S. Const. amend. I because its T-shirts report news and newsworthy information of public interest in which context it is fair to use a public and political figure's image, or (2) Whether Plaintiff is exonerated from liability under Tenn. Code Ann. § 47-25-1107 or U.S. Const. amend. I because its T-shirts are bona fide parodies that are exempt from coverage of the Tennessee Personal Rights Protection Act?

The Tennessee Personal Rights Protection is subject to the protections of the First Amendment. The Tennessee Personal Rights Protection Act provides an exception for the use of a famous image for "news, public affairs" purposes, effectively codifying the aforementioned protections of the First Amendment. Additionally, this Court finds that the First Amendment requires the recognition of a parody exception to the Tennessee Personal Rights Protection Act to protect comment and criticism directed at the famous person whose image is the subject of a bona fide parody. *See generally ETW Corp. v. Jireh Publ'g*, 332 F.3d 915 (6th Cir. 2003) (Ohio statute); *Winter v. DC Comics*, 69 P.3d 473 (Cal. 2003) (Cal. statute); *Comedy III Productions, Inc. v. Gary Saderup, Inc.*, 21 P.3d 797 (Cal. 2001) (Cal. statute); *Cardtoons, L.C. v. MLB Players Assn.*, 95 F.3d 959 (10th Cir. 1996) (Okla. statute).

A. The "News" Exception

The First Amendment protects publication of newsworthy matters or matters of public concern. *See Burson v. Freeman*, 504 U.S. 191 (1992). In order to be exempted, the use of the image must be primarily for conveying information that is neither false nor defamatory and that contributes to the debate of public issues. *See Estate of Elvis Presley v. Russen*, 513 F. Supp. 1339 (D.N.J. 1981). Not every aspect of a person's life, and not everything the person says or does or has said or done in the past automatically is newsworthy or a matter of public interest. *See id.*

The T-shirts in question were sold for purposes of fund raising and for the solicitation of donations. Stip. of Facts ¶ 7. In addition, the shirts bear commercial speech advertising the services and artistic skills of Newsflash Creative Media. They are not related to otherwise protected activities in which the celebrity's image was properly used. The commercial speech involved in this case does not relate back to a valid news publication activity. In addition, the label "Newsflash" is simply a corporate designation, and does not necessarily indicate that the T-shirts are in fact "news" or that they report other matters of public interest.

The T-shirts in question depict the Governor of California in anything but his present status and appearance as governor. Several of the images are from films that were produced more than fifteen years ago, and none of the images depict current events. The fact that three of the images use the word "governor" does not make the images newsworthy as not everything a politician says or does (especially what he said or did fifteen years ago, long before he became governor) can be considered newsworthy and a matter of public interest.

The Court recognizes that the images were not used as actual depictions of current events but rather as a form of commentary on current events – namely Governor Black's interjection into the Tennessee senatorial race of 2004. Certainly coverage of this event is newsworthy and a matter of great public interest, but Newsflash was not covering the event in an effort to disseminate news; their peculiar form of commentary does not fit under the exception carved out for the reporting of news and current events. Nor does the Court find credible Newsflash's allegation that they were engaging in political speech that deserves greater protection under the First Amendment than even the protection extended to news reporting. The creation of a fund raising tool that is both an article of merchandise and a medium to carry commercial speech benefitting Newsflash will not independently stand as political speech merely because the person whose persona is stolen and appropriated for the fund raising and advertising also happens to be a politician. Therefore, Plaintiff are not entitled to the "news" exception.

B. The "Parody" Exception

A bona fide parody that appropriates part of a celebrity's image and persona in an effort to transform the image in a way the casts criticism and ridicule back onto the celebrity can constitute an exempted use of a celebrity's image and persona. *See Winter*, 69 P.3d at 478-79. In applying the "parody" exception to the right of publicity in the context of the visual arts, courts have held that protected parodies are works of art that contain "significant transformative [or creative] elements." *Compare id.* (exception to right of publicity for comic books loosely-based on famous country artists Johnny and Edgar Winter because the Autumn brothers characters—half-human/half-worm creatures with pale faces, red eyes, and long white hair – are unsuitable substitutes for the conventional depictions of the Winter brothers), *and Hoffman v. Capital Cities/ABC, Inc.*, 255 F.3d 1180 (9th Cir. 2000) (exception/defense to right of publicity for computer-altered film still of famous actor Dustin Hoffman from the movie "Tootsie" because Hoffman's long-sleeved, red sequined dress was replaced with a spaghetti-strapped, cream-colored, silk evening dress and high-heeled sandals, and the image also included the following text message: "Dustin Hoffman isn't a drag in a butter-colored silk gown by Richard Tyler and Ralph Lauren heels."), *with Comedy III*, 21 P.3d at 797 (no exception/defense to right of publicity for T-shirts containing signed sketch of Three Stooges because the T-shirts did not contain any transformative or creative elements). The use of the image must relate directly to the protected expression that is communicated; it is not enough that the image accompanies otherwise innocent or protected speech. *See Parks v. LaFace Records*, 329 F.3d 437 (6th Cir. 2003). The celebrity name or likeness must be part and parcel of the protected expression; it cannot simply be used to draw attention to the expression. *See id.*

This Court finds that the instant case is more analogous to *Parks* and *Comedy III.* Plaintiff' T-shirts contain photographs of Black and corresponding messages from his past, nothing more. They do not relate to the expression communicated by Newsflash that the current Governor of California and Republicans in general are not worthy of support by Tennesseans. The use of the images is designed to draw attention to the shirts, nothing more. Nor do the shirts contain any transformative or creative elements. The instant case is distinguishable from *Winter* because only a small part of the Winter brothers' likeness was misappropriated, not their entire image. *Hoffman* also is distinguishable because the court did not focus solely on the text message, but it also focused on other transformative or creative elements – different dress and shoes. Thus, Newsflash is not entitled to the "parody" exception to the right of publicity.

For the reasons stated above, Defendant's Motion for Summary Judgment is granted, and Plaintiff' Motion for Summary Judgment is denied. Plaintiff shall now and henceforth cease and desist to use Defendant's image and likeness on any T-shirt or make any other use of the image in commerce or trade without the consent of Defendant, and Plaintiff shall take steps to retrieve and destroy all existing T-shirts and any other article or merchandise that bears Defendant's image or likeness that Plaintiff created and sold without Defendant's consent.

SO ORDERED, ADJUDGED AND DECREED.

United States District Judge Bernice A. Donald   Date: February 16, 2005

UNITED STATES DISTRICT COURT
WESTERN DISTRICT OF TENNESSEE
WESTERN DIVISION

NEWSFLASH CREATIVE MEDIA,	)	
	)	
Plaintiff,	)	No. 04-C-9345 (BAD)
v.	)	
	)	
ARNOLD BLACK,	)	
	)	
Defendant.	)	

NOTICE OF APPEAL

Notice is hereby given that Plaintiff Newsflash Creative Media hereby appeals to the United States Court of Appeals for the Sixth Circuit from the Order and Judgment entered in this action on the 16th day of February, 2005, granting summary judgment to Defendant Arnold Black and denying summary judgment to Plaintiff.

Date: February 17, 2005

Respectfully submitted,

SERRANO, MAPPLETHORPE, & RODIN, P.C.

By:______________________________

Andres Serrano TN Bar No. 6157980
Robert Mapplethorpe TN Bar No. 6215678
Auguste Rodin TN Bar No. 6223344
139A Beale Street
Memphis, Tennessee 38103
Phone: 800-555-ARTY
Fax: 800-555-SU4U

Attorneys for Plaintiff Newsflash Creative Media

IN THE
UNITED STATES COURT OF APPEALS FOR THE SIXTH CIRCUIT

No. 05-234

NEWSFLASH CREATIVE MEDIA,

Appellant,

v.

ARNOLD BLACK,

Appellee.

Appeal from the United States District Court for the Western District of Tennessee

---

ORDER

The parties in this appeal each shall file their respective briefs (Appellant' brief and Appellee's Brief) on or before 1:30 p.m. on April 4, 2005.

Date: February 17, 2005

____
The Honorable Shania Twain, Chief Judge
